A Source Book of
Buses

A Source Book of
Buses

J. Graeme Bruce

Ward Lock Limited · London

Layout by Viv Harper
House editor Suzanne Kendall
Text photoset in Univers

Set, printed and bound in Great Britain by Netherwood and Dalton, Huddersfield

British Library Cataloguing in Publication Data

Bruce, J. Graeme
  A source book of buses.
  1. Motor buses—History
  I. Title
  629.2'2233   TL232

  ISBN 0-7063-6054-0

Acknowledgments

The author wishes to thank the following for their generous assistance and supply of photographs used in the book: Metro-Cammell Weymann Ltd; Plaxtons of Scarborough; the West Midlands PTE and London Transport, and particular thanks are due to Colin Curtis, John Fielder, David Hunter, Bruce Jenkins, John King, Graham Simons and Arthur Tayler.

The author is also indebted to the Omnibus Society, *Buses*, *Coaching Journal* and *Modern Transport* for the accumulation of knowledge which it is hoped is conveyed in this attempt to give the panoramic view of the bus since its beginnings to the present time. It is hoped that anyone not already fascinated by the subject of buses will be inspired to become interested by reading the pages of this book.

Cover: a restored and privately-owned AEC bus of the early 1930s. Photograph by Peter Wilson for London Transport Executive.

Frontispiece: a rear view of a B type equipped for service with 'bible' type indicator—a feature of London buses for several decades before roller blinds. The length of the vehicle was 5·84 m (19 ft 2 in) and the overall width 2·11 m (6 ft 11 in).

Contents

The horse bus

A horse bus carrying 8 passengers is said to have been operated in Paris in 1662 over a fixed route at a fixed fare by Blaise Pascal and was known as 'carrosse à cinq sous'. Several routes were operated for about twenty years, but they were ahead of their time and fell into disuse. In 1819 Jacques Lafitte introduced a service on routes in Paris, the vehicles were drawn by two horses and carried about 18 passengers. Some of the vehicles were built by an English coachbuilder, George Shillibeer, who had premises in Paris at the time. However, it was Stanislas Baudry who invented the use of the word 'omnibus' to describe his vehicles, which began operating in 1828. He brought the name with him from an operation he had owned in the provincial town of Nantes.

Baudry had been inspired to use the Latin 'omnibus', which could be freely translated as 'by all', to cover a vehicle which picked up and set down in the street, at separate fares, anyone who wished to use the service.

However, by common consent, the continuous history of the 'omnibus' really begins on 4 July 1829 when George Shillibeer began working a 3-horse vehicle between Paddington Green and the Bank in

A replica of George Shillibeer's 3-horse omnibus of 1829. This replica was reconstructed from photographs assuming the dimensions of the horses as no working drawings were available. The replica is now preserved in the Transport Museum at Covent Garden in London.

London, although two years earlier Abraham Brower began working a horse-drawn vehicle seating 12 passengers, which he called 'Accommodation', up and down Broadway in New York at a flat fare irrespective of the distance travelled.

The London route chosen by George Shillibeer was along the New Road outside the area known as 'the stones', which was the congested area with paved streets. This New Road, which follows the line of the present Marylebone Road, was in fact the first 'Ring Road' in London to avoid the built-up area and it was outside the area where hackney coaches had a monopoly for picking up and setting down passengers in the street. Other public conveyances of the day were known as stage coaches but they were required to pre-book and pick up and set down passengers in private yards or premises, frequently public houses or inns. Travel by such vehicles was tedious, time-consuming and rarely undertaken for short distances.

The enterprise of George Shillibeer caused others to engage upon the operation of omnibuses, and the Stage Carriage Act of 1832 authorized the 'plying for hire', that is, the taking up and setting down of passengers on the street by such vehicles, a right which had only previously been accorded to hackney carriages.

The London authorities, however, did not encourage the use of three horses abreast so the horse omnibus settled down to a vehicle designed to be drawn by two horses carrying 18 passengers, 16 in the saloon seated in two rows facing inwards, with 2 other passengers outside seated beside the driver. In the provinces, especially Manchester and Glasgow with rather less congestion than in London, proprietors of omnibuses continued for a number of years to use 3-horse vehicles. The idea of operating horse omnibuses spread rapidly through the country and the description 'omnibus' had come to stay, and gradually by common usage 'bus' entered the English language. Although Shillibeer had decorated the lower side panel of his vehicles with the word 'Omnibus', other proprietors copied this and so, wanting to emphasize his ownership, Shillibeer used his own name, the first use of a fleet name.

The omnibus remained a single-deck vehicle pulled by two horses for a number of years but the process of accommodating passengers on the roof became a natural phenomena of the rush-hour. First of all two or three passengers were accommodated alongside the driver but about 1847 a vehicle was produced with a clerestory roof to the saloon which could be used as a longitudinal roof seat.

The number of vehicles with roof seats increased in 1851 because of the increase in traffic arising from the Great Exhibition in Hyde Park and the vehicles became known as 'knifeboards' because the top-hatted gentlemen sitting back to back looked like sets of black handled knives kept in the racks which were part of the well-equipped kitchens of the time.

At first, access to the roof was by a narrow series of iron tread footholds at the back beside the rear door of the vehicle. The outside seating was no place for ladies for, apart from the difficulty of reaching the seats, their ankles, if nothing else, were exposed to the public gaze. From about 1860 the upper decks were fitted with what were termed 'decency boards' which not only prevented passengers from falling off the roof, but shielded their lower limbs from public examination so that young ladies were no longer discouraged from riding on the top deck. An improved staircase was also provided about this time which made access to the top deck much easier.

In 1855 the London General Omnibus Company (LGOC) was formed, initially in Paris, to consolidate as many of the London omnibus proprietors as possible into one organization and by 1856 three-quarters of the vehicles operating on the London streets had been acquired. The company then set about improving the vehicle and offered a prize for an acceptable design. Although the company gave the award to R. F. Miller of Hammersmith they regretted that out of the 75 designs submitted not one was of

Variant of the knifeboard with a variety of seating arrangements both inside and outside, the precarious iron tread footholds giving access to the roof seats are well defined. It would appear that this vehicle had two doors to the lower saloon—unusual for a London horse bus.

sufficient merit to be accepted unmodified. The basic Miller design accommodated 26 passengers, access to the roof being gained by means of improved steps of metal plates instead of a ringed ladder. At this time the vehicle was not provided with brakes or any communication between the conductor and the driver. The conductor still hung on to a small platform at the rear.

However, as early as 1850 in Manchester the horse bus of the knifeboard type was provided with brakes to the rear wheels and a rope communication with the driver, a device which had been patented in 1847. Variations of this system were still in use on horse buses until 1875 and even later in the motor bus era a string connected to a bell communicated with the driver.

In 1857 the LGOC (the principal bus company in London for almost the next eight decades) began to place new vehicles on the streets of London based on a modified Miller design. They provided back to back knifeboard seating for 10 people, with 2 on each side of the driver giving a top-deck capacity of 14. The inside saloon seating was arranged for 6 on each side facing each other. The width of these vehicles was 1·98 m (6½ ft) overall, a figure which haunted the design of buses for the London streets for many decades. The total capacity of the bus was

Replica of the 'Times' knifeboard-type vehicle used by Thomas Tilling on routes in South London, reasonable staircase and decency boards are now in evidence. The number 393 is the Metropolitan Stage Carriage licence which had to be obtained for every vehicle plying for hire on the streets of London.

thus 26 passengers which became the standard load for two horses. The LGOC eventually had some 600 buses of this type working the London streets, the last one being withdrawn in 1907.

At this time the inside of a bus was lit by smoky oil lamps which were provided not by the company but by the conductor and at night these barely allowed the passengers to see their seats. The speed of the vehicle was about 8 km/h (5 mph) and some journeys were as long as an hour from suburbs such as Hammersmith, Putney and Kilburn to the City, for which the fare was between 4d and 6d in old coinage, the equivalent of 1½p and 2½p today.

In 1881 a new company, the London Road Car Company, began operating horse buses on the London streets in competition with the long established LGOC. This company produced new designs from ideas obtained from the Continent of Europe. They produced a bus with a flat roof instead of a clerestory on which were placed garden seats, two by two, and by 1883 all new London horse buses were of the garden seat type. The vehicle still only carried 26 passengers, 12 inside and 14 outside on pairs of garden seats, the odd pair being beside the stairway. By 1891 40 per cent of the buses operated were the garden seat type. 1901 was the peak year for horse bus operating in London, some 3,736 being

A garden seat-type bus with conductor and driver more or less in uniform.

licensed, and by this time the London vehicle was the lightest and strongest in the world for carrying 28 persons (26 passengers and 2 crew) and the average speed had risen to 13 km/h (8 mph). Standing passengers were not allowed. At this time almost half the number of omnibuses licensed in London were owned by the LGOC.

The last garden seat double-decker horse bus to operate in London was one owned by Thomas Tilling Ltd. on a route between Peckham Rye and Honor Oak on 4 August 1914, the day World War I began for Britain. The last garden seat double-decker horse bus to operate on a regular service in Britain, however, was that worked across the High Level Bridge between Newcastle-on-Tyne and Gateshead and which ended on 13 June 1931.

The horse buses were painted in various colours because it was the practice for each group of routes to be different and for the route indicators themselves to be painted on the vehicles. Although route boards were always carried on the side, the horse bus did not carry a destination plate so that it was often difficult to decide which way the bus was proceeding. In addition to the route board, they carried a sort of fleet name, usually of a geographical nature such as Camden Town, or Putney, but sometimes a true fleet name such as Atlas, Paragon, Favorite and Times. These names indicated the association of proprietors that operated the route, the vehicles carrying the 'fleet names' did not necessarily belong to the same owner, but all worked the same group of routes.

Although the interior of the horse bus was generally lit by a single oil lamp, acetylene and paraffin lamps were now also used. By 1895 brakes were fitted to the rear wheels of horse buses in London, operated by a foot pedal actuated by the driver.

In London a horse bus would run about 100 km (60 miles) a day, but the horses could only cover 19 km (12 miles) in their working day, thus 10 horses were required for each bus on the road. Each horse ate about 7 kg (16 lb) of oats and more than 4 kg (10 lb) of hay each day. The most important official was the vet since his decision was final as to whether the horse was fit for work. The horses in fact cost more to keep than the wages paid to the drivers and conductors.

In the early days of horse bus operation, the wages of the bus crews were usually deducted from the day's takings before these were handed to the owners. Sometimes the conductor had to pay road tolls at toll gates which remained at strategic points in London, such as Notting Hill, Kensington and Islington, until 1864 and a mileage tax was removed in 1869 by the Metropolitan Public Carriage Act. It was about this time, too, that the horse bus stopped crossing from one side of the road to the other to let passengers off as required. This change in practice enabled the provision of a rear platform with access only from the near side.

In addition, the conductor was often required to tip the horse keeper otherwise horse changes were slow or bedevilled by unsatisfactory horses. The 'milking' of the fares was a continuous problem for the proprietors because there was no certain check of the honesty of the conductors.

There was a busmen's strike in 1891 because the LGOC decided to introduce a ticket system on all the routes over which they operated. Tickets had already been introduced by horse tramway systems and by other horse bus operators in various parts of the country, and it was obvious that such systems helped to eliminate fraud. The busmen did achieve, however, a 12 hour day out of the strike although the ticket system was introduced.

The London Road Car Company, when they commenced operating in 1881, had made a ticket system work to their advantage. The system adopted was known as the Bell Punch becoming almost universal as a ticket system in Britain for over 50 years. Individual tickets were issued to each passenger and punched in his or her presence. The conductor's punch retained the circular piece of ticket which in a dispute could be sorted.

The motor bus

The first practical 4-stroke internal combustion engine was invented by Nikolaus Otto in Germany after many years of experimental work. The firm which was organized to exploit his work employed Gottlieb Daimler as production manager and by 1885 he and Karl Benz had produced practical self-propelled cars with engines working on the Otto cycle. The patents taken out by these two men spread to most Western European countries, especially France and England.

The Daimler Motor Company Ltd. was formed in England in 1896, the year that the Locomotive and Highways Act came on to the Statute Book. This was the famous emancipation act which is celebrated each year by the veteran run from London to Brighton by vintage cars. This act, among other things, enabled motor vehicles to travel on the public highway at 19 km/h (12 mph).

The Daimler Company at first imported motor buses from the German Daimler factory at Canstatt but development of the early motor buses using the basic Daimler patents was achieved by another concern which was registered as the Milnes-Daimler Company Ltd. in 1902. Among the first vehicles built by this concern were some single-decker vehicles which were acquired by Eastbourne Corporation for operation in that town. This was the first municipality in Britain to operate motor buses without having previously operated tramcars.

On 17 August 1903 the Great Western Railway began operating motor buses as feeders to their railway system. The first service of this kind being between Helston and the Lizard to avoid the need to build an expensive branch line down the Lizard peninsula. Subsequently a number of Milnes-Daimler double-decker buses were obtained following the showing at the Crystal Palace Motor Show of 1904 of such a vehicle with an 18 kW (24 hp) engine.

Between 1905 and 1907 a large number of pioneer motor bus operations began using Milnes-Daimler vehicles, not only in London but in the provinces. By the end of 1907 over 300 Milnes-Daimler double-decker buses were working on the streets of London, mostly owned by a new operating company called the London Motor Omnibus Co. Ltd. who had adopted the fleet name 'Vanguard', in fact the first use of a specific fleet name instead of a route, operator, or area name. This company appreciated the worth of the Milnes-Daimler and obtained a first option on all double-deckers constructed until 1907 which made it difficult for other operators to purchase them. The Vanguard was very progressive

The first Milnes-Daimler owned by the Great Western Railway seated 22 passengers in a wagonette-type body. The engine developed 12 kW (16 hp).

and was the first to adopt route numbers in London because the use of a fleet name virtually killed the route name.

The Heavy Motor Car Order produced under the Motor Car Act 1903 provided that a commercial vehicle 'shod' (note the horse bus terminology) with rubber tyres on all wheels, should have an unladen weight of 5 tons and not exceed a width of 2·18 m (7 ft 2 in) and could travel on the public highway at 19 km/h (12 mph).

The London and North Western Railway began bus feeder services in the Harrow and Watford areas on the outskirts of London. They obtained specially-built Milnes-Daimlers which could be claimed as the first purpose-built motor buses in England.

The Milnes-Daimler built in 1905 had a 4-speed gearbox driving the rear wheels by chain, but which was disengaged from the engine by means of a cone clutch. The engine had 4 cylinders being described by the convention of the time as 12 kW (16 hp).

A Bristol firm of engineers, which in 1905 became Sidney Straker and Squire Ltd., manufactured vehicles known as Straker-Squires. A manufacturing agreement with the German firm of Büssing to construct motor buses designed to their patents was arranged.

The Büssing concern turned out their first motor bus in 1904, eventually supplying numerous vehicles for Berlin and other cities. The London market, however, was at this time the most buoyant and every manufacturer of commercial vehicles was anxious to sell for operation in London.

The London Road Car Company who adopted the fleet name 'Union Jack' considered the Straker-Squire bus of 1905 the most suitable vehicle for horse bus replacement. The drive of these early

A Milnes-Daimler with a special body which includes a luggage compartment directly behind the driver, obtained in 1906 by London and North Western Railway for service between Harrow and Watford.

Straker-Squires was by means of side chains from an intermediate gearbox which had six forward gears and two reverse. The system was noisy and led to the loss of the popularity of this vehicle; however, by 1908 the Straker-Squire was the most numerous of makes on the London streets and together with Milnes-Daimler types, accounted for more than half the 1,000 motor buses then operating in the metropolis.

The regulations imposed by the Metropolitan Police concerning motor buses in London at the time were very rigid. These regulations required that the wheelbase should not exceed 4·42 m (14½ ft), the length overall was limited to 7 m (23 ft), with the width not exceeding 2·18 m (7 ft 2 in), the seating being limited to 18 passengers on top and 16 inside. The Straker-Squire actually had an overall length of 5·87 m (19¼ ft) with a width of barely 2·13 m (7 ft).

In the first ten years, therefore, the motor bus scene was dominated by two basically German designed vehicles, although there were also the Swiss Orions, French De Dions, Belgian Germain and German Durkopp, interested in the market. British names such as Maudslay, Wolseley, Arrol-Johnston, Leyland-Crossley, Thornycroft, Scott-Stirling and Dennis then appeared on the London streets; other manufacturers, however, were not interested in the London market because of the severe weight and size restrictions imposed by the Metropolitan Police.

The work of the two Frenchmen Georges Bouton and Count Albert De Dion led to the development of a lightweight high-speed internal combustion engine incorporating the Daimler master patents but their achievement was really based upon the provision of a reliable ignition system.

The first De Dion motor bus appeared in London in 1905 and was adopted by the General as the best vehicle to meet their requirements since the Milnes-Daimler was virtually unavailable to them because of the sales monopoly already held by Vanguard. At the Olympia Motor Show of 1907 the De Dion Bouton which was exhibited was powered by a 4-cylinder engine developing about 22 kW (30 brake horse power). De Dion Bouton introduced forced engine lubrication and a leather faced cone friction clutch. Another feature of the De Dion design was the provision of a differential in a counter shaft with half shafts driving each wheel on a rigid rear axle to reduce the noise arising from the more usual chain drive.

In 1905 the well established Wolseley Tool and Motor Car Company introduced a bus chassis for a 36-seater double-deck body, using a 2-cylinder horizontal engine and side chain drive. This design allowed the driver to sit virtually on top of the engine, an early design of what became later known as forward control. This engine was soon replaced by a vertical 4 cylinder design although the final drive was still by twin chains one to each wheel from a differential shaft. The Wolseley engine had separate individual cylinder blocks each of which could be removed and changed separately.

The first Dennis appeared in 1906 and was provided with a worm drive back axle which finally dispensed with the need to use noisy chains for the final drive. This arrangement was in fact a major contribution to the development of the bus.

Christopher Dodson, originally a builder of horse buses, began constructing motor bus bodies which met the Metropolitan Police regulations but were standardized to fit a variety of chassis. By introducing route numbers the Vanguard Company had avoided the need to paint the vehicles different colours for the different routes which had been the horse bus practice. Christopher Dodson introduced removable destination boards as part of the body structure. These boards not only provided the ultimate destination in bold letters, but some of the important places en route. It was a small step to introduce the 'bible' type indicator which could be turned over so that the intermediate places were in direction order, (see frontispiece). This type became a feature of the London motor bus and some provincial operations as well. It now became the practice to adopt a fleet name for all vehicles rather than a route name. The fleet name 'General' was adopted by the largest London operator in 1905.

The great bus amalgamation in London became effective on 1 July 1908 when the fleets of the Vanguard, the Road Car and the General concerns were welded into an enlarged London General Omnibus Co. Ltd. The Vanguard at this time contributed twice as many motor buses to the joint fleet as the old General. It was not until 1910, however, that the number of motor buses licensed in London at a total of 1,142 exceeded the number of horse buses licensed. After this, however, the demise of the horse bus was rapid. By 25 October 1911 the last General horse bus had been withdrawn and the last horse bus owned by an independent operator, Thomas Tilling Ltd. ceased working on 4 August 1914.

The Vanguard having begun as a motor bus concern right from the start had established an engineering works in Walthamstow in 1906. An experimental design of bus was produced by the new LGOC which incorporated the best features of the De Dion

The B type—the first standard London motor bus seated 16 passengers inside and 18 outside. Many vehicles of this type were impressed for service in Flanders during World War I. 'Old Bill', one of these vehicles, is preserved in the Imperial War Museum and another is in the London Transport Museum at Covent Garden.

Milnes-Daimler, Wolseley and Straker-Squire vehicles of which the combined fleet of the amalgamated company was made up. The first of these experimental vehicles appeared in 1909.

Arising from the operation of this experimental type came the famous 'B' type of which a total of nearly 3,000 were built, the first appearing on the streets of London in October 1910. In 1912 the manufacturing business of the General was transferred to a new company, the Associated Equipment Co. Ltd. and the famous AEC marque was born. This company continued to produce buses for over 50 years not only for London but for all over the world. Initially, however, the Associated Equipment Company was forbidden by its deed of incorporation to sell buses directly to any operator within 48 km (30 miles) of Charing Cross, other than the London General Omnibus Company.

The B type vehicle was provided with a 22 kW (30 hp) 4-cylinder engine which was constructed with a 'T' head having side valves and a magneto provided the ignition. This vehicle still used a cone clutch and a 4-speed gearbox eliminating the final noisy chain drive to the rear wheels.

In 1909 the Police Regulations for buses operating in London were such that the unladen weight was restricted to 3½ tons with not more than 4 tons of the laden weight of 6 tons to be on the rear axle. The B type was provided with brakes on the rear wheels only of the internally expanding shoe type operating on drums. In addition a hand-brake working on the transmission was also provided. The speed of a motor bus at this time was restricted to 19 km/h (12 mph).

The B type vehicle was generally equipped with single solid tyres on the front wheels and twin solid tyres on the rear wheels. The B type chassis was the first commercial vehicle in Britain to be built on a production line. By June 1911, 20 vehicles were being produced per week and this high rate enabled the LGOC to withdraw the remaining horse bus services very quickly. By 1912 the rate of production had increased to 30 chassis a week.

The factors that influenced the development of electric transmission was the ease of operation, the reduction in noise, and freedom from fatigue so far as the driver was concerned. In England this was helpful in training horse bus drivers to operate motor buses while in America it was helpful in re-training electric tramcar drivers.

The petrol-electric drive found more favour in the United States than in Europe. It had several advantages, such as smooth acceleration with less strain on the engine which ran basically at a constant

speed, a speed which suited the engine. There was little wear and tear on transmission since this was carried over electrical connections rather than by mechanical means, the actual road drive being completed by one or two traction motors driving the back wheels. There were some disadvantages, for example, increased weight leading to increased fuel consumption. Another disadvantage, was the absence of the engine as a brake so there was increased wear on the brake liners which led the American designers to introduce powered air brakes long before this became the practice in Britain.

After several types of petrol-electric vehicles had been produced in Britain, Thomas Tilling Ltd., the London bus operator became interested in its further development because, like other operators, they had found difficulties with the proprietary buses being sold on the market. They considered that neither the Milnes-Daimler, Straker-Squire nor

The twin-motor drive of the Yellow Coach double-decker buses of Philadelphia in 1925. A 6-cylinder petrol engine placed in the conventional forward position drove an electric generator, the drive to each rear wheel was by means of a separate electric motor. This system eliminated the gearbox and differential.

Dennis vehicles, which they were already operating on the London streets, was entirely suitable for replacing their 220 horse buses. They decided that a petrol-electric transmission was much easier for horse bus drivers to be taught the new techniques of controlling a mechanically propelled vehicle because there was no troublesome gearbox.

The firm of Tilling-Stevens Ltd. was then formed in 1906 to manufacture vehicles with a petrol-electric transmission system for bus operation. The first production design of this concern was the TTA1 which appeared in 1911. The drive was by means of a series motor through a cardan shaft to worm gearing on a live back axle. On the original models the radiator was mounted behind the 22 kW (30 hp) engine covered with a 'coal scuttle' cover. The 4-cylinder engine was directly coupled to a generator through a flexible coupling. The body was based on the horse bus garden seat-type seating 34 passengers. The first production TTA1 began operating for Thomas Tilling Ltd. on 11 June 1911.

Tilling-Stevens continued to build petrol-electric vehicles until 1926 when the development of the friction clutch and mechanical transmission system were such that not only a smoother acceleration was possible, but the fuel consumption was much improved with the conventional arrangement.

Petrol-electric transmissions were particularly useful where conversion from tramway to bus was undertaken. Leicester Corporation in 1924-5 obtained a small fleet of both single and double-deckers. The photograph shows a TS6 with Brush bodywork seating 24 upstairs and 26 downstairs.

After World War I

At the end of World War I a number of men came back from the forces trained to drive heavy vehicles and with plenty of war surplus vehicles available it was natural that many should turn to providing a bus service in various parts of the country where there was a growing need for greater individual mobility. Many proprietors owned only one or two vehicles, often driving themselves. These individual proprietors found the need to co-operate and joined bus operating associations which looked after their interests on a sharing basis but the need for their continuation disappeared as the smaller proprietors were acquired by larger organizations.

In the early days to meet the needs of these owner-drivers, several small cheap vehicles, mainly of foreign manufacture, appeared on the market: Reo, Chevrolet, Graham and Dodge coming from the USA in large numbers, Lancia and Fiat from Italy and Berliet from France were among the most popular. They were usually fitted with 19, 20 or 26-seater bodies. In fact the Model T Ford which first appeared in 1911, (the most famous motor vehicle chassis of all time and which remained in mass production until 1927) was also used to provide small buses. This commercial version was produced by extending the

Typical of the extended car chassis adapted for a small bus body in the early 1920s is this 14-seater Chevrolet for service with the Great Western Railway.

chassis giving either a 381 kg or 1016 kg (7½ cwt or 20 cwt) version. Both versions were powered by a 4-cylinder 15 kW (20 hp) engine coupled to a multi-disc clutch and 2-speed gearbox. In 1921 the long wheel based model was imported to Britain and subsequently assembled at a new factory established at Trafford Park, Manchester. Such a vehicle,

The Scottish commercial vehicle manufacturing concern Albion produced many types of buses until the company was absorbed by Leyland in 1951. The forward control low-loading type, introduced about 1927, became very popular with many operators. Shown is a Scottish Motor Traction version which had a rear-entrance and seats for 29.

seating 20 passengers, was exhibited at the Commercial Motor Show of 1921. In fact the Model T Ford was the first of numerous small-capacity buses imported from abroad immediately after World War I, beginning the extraordinary expansion of the bus industry in Britain—an expansion which was far greater than in any other country in the world. The Reo Speed Wagon with a 14-seater body appeared in 1924 with pneumatic tyres, a later version was the Reo Pullman which was provided with a 6-cylinder engine and seats for 26 and these became very popular with small proprietors in Scotland.

Leyland Motors Ltd., who were already well-established as the builders of buses, were concerned that they were unable to obtain a foothold in London because of the virtual monopoly by AEC and Tilling-Stevens but developed the LB (London Bus) type to conform to Metropolitan Police Regulations. A number of independent proprietors obtained Leyland buses of this type to start in competition with the established General and other operators. In 1922 Arthur George Partridge, the first of the independents who soon became known as 'pirates', introduced the Chocolate Express. The London Traffic Act of 1924 eventually came into being to bring order out of the chaos, because by 1925 there were over 500 buses operating in London, mostly double-deckers, not associated with the General and taking the cream of the traffic. The Leyland LB type had a transmission brake as well as brake shoes on drums on each rear wheel. Leyland vehicles of similar design were sold in large numbers to provincial operators outside London.

Under the London Traffic Act of 1924 the vehicles themselves were limited among many other requirements to an unladen weight on 4 wheels of 7¼ tons or 10 tons on 6 wheels. Single-deckers were permitted to have a length of 8·38 m (27½ ft) on 4 wheels, while double-deckers were not permitted to exceed 8 m (26 ft). On the other hand vehicles on 6 wheels could have a length of 9·14 m (30 ft). The maximum overall width at this time was still restricted to 2·29 m (7½ ft).

Double-deckers continued to be built with open tops on 4-wheeled chassis within the legal weight limits which were governed by the Town Police Clauses Acts and the Heavy Motor Car Acts. In London, however, the width was restricted by the Metropolitan Police to 2·18 m (7 ft 2 in) until 1928. These were onerous restrictions and reduced to some extent the usefulness of double-deckers which were not only very economical in road occupation but carried more passengers. Another factor which retarded the development of double-deckers for

The Leyland SG7 produced in 1922 with the driver beside the engine. Ribble Motor Services were among the first to operate a fleet of these vehicles.

A 1920 Leyland in the fleet of Edinburgh Corporation subsequently fitted with pneumatic tyres.

services other than for heavy duty urban traffic, was the difficulty of fitting pneumatic tyres, known at the time as 'balloon' tyres, because of weight problems.

In 1923, however, a major step in London bus design had been the 'NS' which was provided with a

In London the 'K' type appeared in 1919 being built right out to the 2·18 m (7 ft 2 in) width limitation enabling 2 × 2 seating to be fitted in the lower saloon. The length of the vehicle was under 7 m (23 ft) but the driver was placed in the forward control position over the engine.

An open-top NS with solid tyres and an overall length of 8 m (26 ft), and a laden weight just over 9 tons. More than 2,000 of this type were built for operation in London.

low centre of gravity with a view to it being fitted with a covered top. The first one began operating without this amenity and it was not until 1925 that covered tops were permitted. This vehicle originally had solid tyres, but in 1928 they began to be fitted with pneumatic tyres, but again the regulation had to be amended because the fitting of 'balloon' tyres to the NS caused it to exceed the 2·18 m (7 ft 2 in) width by about 4 cm (1½ in).

On 1 October 1928, when the Ministry of Transport raised the speed limit of buses fitted with pneumatic tyres to 32 km/h (20 mph) all new vehicles in Britain were, in fact, being fitted with pneumatics.

In 1925 General Motors Corporation of America acquired the old established firm of Vauxhall Motors Ltd. of Luton. In 1931 an 'all British' model, given the name Bedford, was produced which at first resembled the Chevrolet. By this time the importation of buses had virtually ceased, partly because the production of British-built buses was meeting the need and partly because of the heavy tax on motor vehicle imports.

This was a time of intense competition because in Britain prior to 1930 the licensing and regulations of omnibuses plying for hire was covered by the Town Police Clauses Act of 1847 modified in 1889. This Act was originally designed to safeguard the public from, among other matters, unscrupulous hackney carriage proprietors. The right to apply these Acts in any area was contained in the bye-laws of various local authorities. Not all local authorities bothered to take advantage of the powers conferred on them by the Act but, nevertheless, by 1930 there were some 1,300 authorities in Britain which had acquired the right to control hackney carriages by a licensing system which included buses, picking up and setting down on the public highway. Adjacent licensing authorities would licence different proprietors and then their buses would run on the return ticket principle in competition with each other. The police were then required to prosecute the offenders and *agents provocateurs* were employed to catch operators infringing the licensing arrangements. This problem was solved by the 1930 Road Traffic Act which divided the country into Traffic Areas with Commissioners given wide powers concerning vehicle standards and route operation, together with the granting of licences, a system which stood the test of time for fifty years before any major amendment was considered desirable. A trial of the basis of the system had been achieved by the 1924 London Traffic Act which regulated buses in London but only covered the Metropolitan Area.

The years of development 1925-45

The first important development was the design of a chassis specially for buses, instead of being adopted from a truck chassis. The most outstanding development in this field was the Leyland Titan TD1 which first appeared in 1927. Two-axle double-deckers were restricted at this time to a maximum length of 8 m (26 ft) and as balloon tyres were not yet of adequate strength to carry a fully-laden conventional 4-wheeled double-decker, the development of 6-wheelers was begun to spread the load.

Leyland, however, produced a lightweight double-deck body with a low overall height to fit a specially designed low cranked chassis on two axles. In fact this was the first time in Britain that a body and chassis had been designed as a unit, although it could be claimed that the original London B type almost achieved this in 1911. The overall height was kept low by access to the seats on the top deck being arranged from a sunken gangway on the off side from the stairwell to the front. The bottom of this gangway protruded into the lower saloon so that passengers sitting in the seats below were warned to mind their head. This design reduced the height of the conventional double-decker at that time by as much as 1 m (3 ft).

Glasgow Corporation ordered 112 of the TD1 lowbridge vehicle from Leyland for delivery in 1928. It was the largest single order placed for these vehicles and enabled the Corporation to inaugurate a network of bus routes supplementary to the extensive tramway system then operating in Glasgow.

The classic Leyland photograph showing the TD1 of 1927 on pneumatic tyres with 4 m (13 ft) lowbridge body alongside a Leviathan-type constructed only 2 years earlier.

was about 4 m (13 ft), and the design became known as the 'lowbridge' type as a more conventional 'highbridge', or normal height double-decker, was built subsequently. The 'lowbridge' bus, however, became enormously popular, revitalizing the use of double-deckers in Britain not only for urban routes, but for country services as well.

Because the chassis was cranked between the axles, the floor level of the lower saloon was only 711 mm (2 ft 4 in) above ground level, so that by making the platform only 356 mm (1 ft 2 in) from the road level an easy entrance was possible. Aluminium was used in the body construction which enabled the weight of the complete unladen bus to be kept down to about 5½ tons thus allowing the fitting of pneumatic tyres. The top deck was extended over the driver's cab, a feature which previously had not been standard practice. The TD1 was provided with a 6-cylinder overhead camshaft 6·8 litre petrol engine and the braking was vacuum servo assisted.

The next important development was the diesel engine. Up to this time, apart from a limited number of steam driven and battery-operated vehicles, all buses had been powered by petrol engines. As early as 1908 at the Saurer works in Switzerland, Rudolf Diesel had completed the first high speed diesel

The seating arrangement was 51, 24 in the lower saloon and 27 in the upper in six rows of 4 with the rear row only taking 3 passengers. The overall height

engine suitable for commercial vehicles. The German company Maschinenfabrik Augsburg-Nürnberg (MAN) was the first engineering firm to construct compression ignition engines in quantity to the designs of Rudolf Diesel and in 1924 began to manufacture them for use on commercial vehicles.

The merger of the German Daimler and Benz organizations in 1924, produced the famous Mercedes marque of commercial vehicles and they developed a diesel engine to power them. By 1932 this organization was producing over 2,000 diesel engines annually for commercial vehicles and one or two of these engines were tried experimentally in Britain by various manufacturers and operators.

However, one of the characteristics of the Gardner diesel engine manufactured in England was its low fuel consumption and its ease of substitution for contemporary petrol engines. Between 1932 and 1934 many engines of this type were fitted to different vehicles by many operators for experimental purposes. In 1934 Guy Motors was the first manufacturer to fit Gardner engines exclusively to their buses in preference to petrol engines.

One of the interesting features of the Gardner range of engines was the provision of a 5-cylinder in-line motor. A 5-cylinder arrangement had practically been unknown in automobile practice up to that time. Such engines actually provided sufficient power to replace 6-cylinder contemporary petrol engines without having to make any drastic change in the chassis. When more power was required by buses during World War II dispensation was given to allow vehicles to exceed the legal overall length by extending the radiator a little so that they could be fitted with the 6-cylinder diesel engines. Many operators were introduced to the Gardner engine by the use of these wartime buses, and as they proved very reliable they were pleased to accept the engine subsequently after the war. The Gardner engine is still being specified in its modern form by many operators.

The Bristol Tramways Co. designed its first chassis in 1908 after being dissatisfied with the contemporary vehicle manufactured. The Tilling organization obtained control of the Bristol Co. in 1935 including the manufacturing business and thereafter encouraged its subsidiary operating concerns to buy Bristol vehicles usually fitted with Eastern Coach Work bodies. Eastern Coach Works at Lowestoft started in 1912 as part of the United Automobile Service Ltd. to build bodies for that company's buses. Subsequently the body building business was formed into a separate company as the Eastern Coach Works Ltd.

A Guy Arab originally provided, in 1949, with a 5-cylinder Gardner engine and wartime utility body. In 1952 Southdown replaced these with an open-top body and a 6-cylinder Gardner engine requiring the radiator to be mounted further forward.

A new 3 ton Bedford chassis was introduced in 1934 on which a 26-seater bus body could be fitted. This was the first Bedford to employ the semi-forward position. Although a bonneted front appearance was presented externally the engine protruded back into the body beside the driver. This vehicle became very popular with many operators. Vacuum assisted servo brakes on all 4 wheels were now provided as standard on all buses.

In 1939 the OB type Bedford with a wheel base of 4·42 m (14½ ft), a 4-cylinder engine and conventional gearbox, was placed on the market. This chassis was accepted by the Ministry of Supply as the basis for a utility wartime vehicle and a 32-seater body was designed for it which could be produced by any orthodox vehicle builder. Such vehicles were the only new single-decker buses produced in Britain during the 1942-5 war period.

In 1928 the four main line railway companies received bus operating powers and very sensibly did not set up to compete with existing operators, but entered into financial arrangements with the large companies already established as well as municipal operators with whom they arranged joint ownership of the bus operations. Huddersfield, Halifax and Sheffield Corporations became involved in this way. One or two companies subsequently entered into

A Bedford Duple Sportsman of 1951 in the famous MacBrayne livery. This pleasing design of a 20-seater bus for one-man operation was very popular with many operators.

A Bristol Lodekka in the fleet of the jointly-operated Keighley-West Yorkshire service, an organization partly private and partly municipal.

agreements also with municipalities for joint ownership of the service. The Keighley-West Yorkshire Service Ltd., for example, was formed in 1932. Other municipalities leased or sold their operation to the company operating in their area.

The 1930 Road Traffic Act which gave, among other things, security of tenure to existing operators, enabled consolidations to be arranged which strengthened the operation of the big groups. The companies in these big groups rarely competed with one another and became known as 'area agreement' companies.

The powers given to the main line railways to enter the bus operating field was not granted too soon because bus competition for long-distance operation began about the same time. Greyhound Motors Ltd. of Bristol receive the credit for inaugurating the first regular long-distance service rather than an excursion type bus service between London and Bristol in 1925. It should be borne in mind that until October 1928 the maximum speed applying to buses and coaches was 19 km/h (12 mph) so that long-distance operation was very slow unless the law was defied.

The first rigid 6-wheeled passenger vehicle was developed in the United States, not by a vehicle builder, but by the Goodyear Tire and Rubber Company of Akron in order to prove that pneumatic tyres could be used with heavy duty vehicles. By 1918 pneumatic tyres of very large dimensions were available but by spreading the weight over 3 axles instead of 2, thereby reducing the weight on individual wheels, a smaller type of pneumatic tyre could be used.

Until 1925 there were very few 6-cylinder engines in use on buses in Britain and there had been very few 6-wheelers. Büssing in Germany had produced a 6-wheeled chassis in 1923, the first 3-axle bus to be produced in that country. Both rear wheels were driven, the motor used being a 6-cylinder 45 kW (60 hp) machine. A large number of Continental, particularly German operators, obtained Büssing buses and until they went out of fashion, this manufacturer produced about 98 per cent of the Continental requirements of this type.

Guy Motors created a sensation in 1926 by also producing a 6-wheeled double-decker. This was not only the first double-decker produced by this concern, but it actually appeared before any other 6-wheeler in Britain. It was provided with a 4-cylinder engine and was rather under-powered, but it had some success, however, with independent operators in London and others in the provinces.

In 1929 AEC produced three related chassis including the Renown which was a 6-wheeled version and could be provided with a single-decker body 9·14 m (30 ft) long or a double-decker 8·23 m (27 ft) long. The first double-deckers for London on this chassis, designated LT type, were provided with bodies having an outside staircase, and for the first time in London it was arranged that the driver could be protected from the weather by a glass windscreen.

The LS type was the first 6-wheeler to be operated by the predecessors of London Transport and all except LS6 were double-deckers. Even in 1927 the driver's protection was meagre due to Metropolitan Police requirements. LS6 was unique in that it was provided for a time with petrol-electric transmission and a Daimler sleeve valve engine.

The LT type, constructed by AEC between 1929 and 1932 for operation in London, had various versions of body—some seating 60 but the majority of double-deckers seated 56. A total of 1,400 was built including some single-deckers. The overall height was 4·27 m (14 ft) and the length 8·23 m (27 ft).

The 6-wheeled vehicle for normal passenger work was halted in its development in Britain when there was a relaxation in the 4-wheeled vehicle dimensions. In 1937 Leyland produced the Gnu chassis with the twin axles at the front with twin steering within the 9·14 m (30 ft) permitted length, but very few of these unorthodox vehicles were produced. However, in 1962 Bedford produced a 6-wheeled type of chassis with twin steering front wheels with the engine in the conventional position ahead of the front axle. The 3 axles were no longer required to achieve vehicle length because the law now allowed the dimensions to be 11 m (36 ft) long and 2·5 m (8 ft 2½ in) wide. The arrangement was considered to provide a safer type of vehicle for high speeds on motorways. Production of this type ceased in 1971 and 6-wheeled vehicles are now rare in Britain.

The 3-axle bus found favour again in America when the Greyhound Corporation designed the first Scenicruiser. It was constructed in collaboration with General Motors, being a vehicle 12·2 m (40 ft) long instead of 10·67 m (35 ft) of previous design, and had a raised rear level making it almost a deck-and-a-half vehicle. It was provided with exceptional baggage capacity and a lavatory. The extra baggage capacity was used by Greyhound to increase the express package service.

Twin-steering Leyland Gnu produced in 1937 gave a different wheel arrangement for a 9·14 m (30 ft) coach which did not find a great deal of favour.

The Bedford VAL produced in 1962 was a 6-wheeled chassis with the twin axles at the front, both steerable. The vehicle was 11 m (36 ft) long and 2·5 m (8 ft 2½ in) wide. Shown is a Duple-bodied vehicle from the fleet of the London coach and tour operator, Grey Green Coaches.

The first prototype Scenicruiser went into service in 1949 but it was 1954 before 1,000 were ordered. The vehicle was provided with air suspension and two 4-cylinder engines driving the rear axle through a fluid coupling and single transmission.

Engines and transmission

The early buses which were not developments from the private car just before World War I had 4-cylinder petrol engines, magneto ignition and a 4-speed gearbox, with the final drive to the rear axle being by chain developing about 30 hp (22 kW) calculated by what was known as the R.A.C. rating. It was not until about 1925 that engines started to be described by the swept volume or capacity of the cylinders in litres or cubic centimetres.

In 1902 C. Y. Knight, an American engineer, took out a patent in the United States for a sleeve valve engine, that is, an engine which opens and closes the gas ports of the cylinders by means of sleeves instead of by the more conventional means of poppet valves raised by cams. At the time of this development most engines were considered to be very noisy but the sleeve valve engine ran very quietly.

In 1906 the Daimler Company in England acquired the manufacturing rights to the system. Production began in 1908 and sleeve valve engines continued to be manufactured by the Daimler Company until 1933. Later the Daimler sleeve valve engine was manufactured in America under licence for use initially in the New York and Chicago double-decker

Minerva Motors of Belgium manufactured the 'Silent Knight' sleeve valve engine and the S.M.T. in Scotland, who began building their own buses in 1918, used this engine. The first Lothian had a very unorthodox appearance with a large 'coal-scuttle' front. Later a more conventional full front forward control was adopted, one of the first forward control designs which subsequently became standard practice in bus design.

Not quite an orthodox engine-gearbox-differential chassis because the whole drive has been offset to provide a low floor height and additional space for an entrance. The chassis is a Yellow Coach model of about 1924 for New York. *Left*

A Versare of 1927—a vehicle of very advanced design—an integral 6-wheeled vehicle with what was termed a 'street car' body. A 6-cylinder engine placed transversely at the rear drove an electric generator. Two electric motors drove each pair of rear wheels through differential gears. This was the first bus design to provide an entrance in front of the front wheels. Production ceased in 1931 when the manufacturer was acquired by an established tramcar builder. *Below*

buses. The factory concerned with their construction eventually became part of the Yellow Truck and Coach Company and subsequently the General Motors Corporation.

Until about 1925 bus engines remained of 4 cylinders up to a maximum of about 37 kW (50 hp). The transmission was either by cardan shaft from a 4-speed gearbox to a differential or worm gear on the back axle or by what was termed electric transmission where the engine drove a generator and an electric motor drove the cardan shaft to the back axle. This was known as the petrol-electric drive favoured in America more than in Britain where only one concern, Tilling-Stevens, successfully exploited the system. General Motors in America claimed in 1928 that they were the pioneers of the modern electrical transmission system and offered such a system as an alternative to the straight-forward mechanical arrangement. In fact all the buses operating in Philadelphia in 1928, a fleet of several hundred, had petrol-electric transmissions and at this time most of the American chassis manufacturers were prepared to offer this system as an alternative to the clutch and gearbox arrangement.

The preselective gearbox appeared in 1930, at first it was applied to Daimler private cars and then to Daimler public service vehicles. The driver selected the gear in advance, which was not engaged until the driver pressed his foot pedal. The Wilson preselective gearbox was then adopted for fitting to AEC buses for London.

In order to meet the competition that this improvement in transmission made, Leyland introduced a torque convertor in 1933. Buses were sold using this system under the term 'Gearless'. There was no clutch pedal and this was almost a fully automatic system with only a lever to select direct drive not through the torque convertor above 32 km/h (20 mph). This system, however, did not prove to be economical and was not generally accepted in Britain although it found favour in America, especially where rear engines were fitted.

As long ago as 1937 experiments began in providing automatic gear changing for buses. A gearbox with mechanical selection was arranged so that this selection could be activated electrically and the movement performed by compressed air. Development of this equipment was interrupted by World War II.

After the war the Self Changing Gear Company, which had been formed to exploit the arrangement, designed a new gearbox in which gear change was effected by hydraulic pressure. A semi-automatic gear changing arrangement of this kind was applied

to a number of buses from 1948. This arrangement combined the preselective gearbox with an automatic gear change up or down from the gear selected. This ensured that the engine braking facility required for downhill operation of buses would still be available.

In 1935 Midland Red produced a rear-engined single-decker with a petrol engine mounted transversely behind the rear axle, followed in 1940 by an underfloor engine placed horizontally behind the front wheels, but development was halted by the war. These developments were made by operating concerns and not chassis manufacturers. Midland Red, of course, had been manufacturing some of its own vehicles since 1923.

In 1932 the Northern General produced a side-engine design which in the 4-wheeled version provided seats for 40 passengers in the 8·38 m (27½ ft) length—a high capacity for a single decker at this time.

In 1932 this revolutionary design was produced for service in London. The AEC Q type had a diesel engine mounted slightly inclined on the off side of the chassis. This positioning of the engine enabled the whole of the body floor to be utilized for passengers so that as many as 37 passengers could be seated within the width of 2·29 m (7½ ft) and 8·38 m (27½ ft) length. The production models of this type were all single-deckers with all-metal bodywork and many had front-entrance bodies built by Park Royal Vehicles Ltd.

The standard double-decker bus in London in the early 1930s was the AEC LT type and this was used to experiment with various arrangements of petrol and diesel engines, crash and preselective gearboxes, as well as vacuum servo and Lockheed hydraulic brakes. The LT was an elongated version of the T type single-decker on 6 wheels to enable the vehicle to have a length of 9·14 m (30 ft). The ST type was the 4-wheeled version which in 1929 could only be built to a length of 7·6 m (25 ft) and therefore only carried 48 passengers. The formation of London Transport on 1 July 1933 caused the AEC organization to become a separate entity but the vehicle designs continued to be oriented round the requirements for service in London.

Early in 1932 the M.O.T. relaxed the wheelbase dimensions of a 4-wheeled double-decker enabling a 60-seater body to be provided within the 8 m (26 ft) overall length. The standard London bus of this period, the STL, took advantage of this as well as the change from petrol engines and crash gearboxes to oil engines and self-changing gearboxes.

The first British production designed vehicle with an engine having an underfloor mounting. The prototype TF1 appeared in 1937 for Green Line service with London Transport. The engine was a Leyland 6-cylinder diesel with a flat construction, transmission was by AEC fluid flywheel and preselective gearbox. The overall length was 8·38 m (27½ ft) and width 2·29 m (7½ ft).

In 1948 Sentinel produced the integral bus (the STC4 model) which had a limited acceptance, Commer then produced an underfloor-engined bus with the engine at the front almost in the conventional position. However, it was not until 1950 that the change in regulations enabled the engine position to be moved from the established arrangement at the front. American engineers had produced underfloor designs several decades earlier, the Fageol Twin Coach had appeared in 1928.

In 1950 the AEC Regal IV was produced with a horizontally-mounted engine. At about the same time Leyland, together with Metro-Cammell-Weymann introduced the Olympic, at first restricted in size by the regulations, but subsequently produced 9·14 m × 2·44 m (30 ft × 8 ft). This was one of the first integral buses built by a bodybuilder with Leyland components. It also had a horizontal engine.

These vehicles were followed by underfloor designs from other chassis manufacturers and Foden produced a rear-engined design transversely mounted in 1950, a type of design which was already well established in America, the Mack C50, for example, produced for operation in New York in 1948.

The Leyland Atlantean first appeared in 1956, the first double-decker to go into mass production with

The Sentinel-Beadle was produced between 1948 and 1957 by the collaboration of a vehicle manufacturer and a coachbuilder and over 500 examples of this integral bus were delivered to small operators. The Sentinel Company became part of the Rolls-Royce organization and production ceased.

The Twin Coach developed by Fageol had two small 6-cylinder petrol engines on either side of the chassis behind the front axle. The subsequent transmission to the rear wheels could either be mechanical through twin gearboxes and separate cardan shafts (each side being virtually independent) or by electric transmission, the engines driving generators with twin motors attached to separate driving shafts. *Right*

The Mack C50 approximately 12·2 m (40 ft) long of integral construction having a transverse mounted 6-cylinder diesel engine at the rear driving the back axle through a torque convertor. The bus could carry 80 passengers of which 48 were provided with seats. A special feature of the design was the provision of 'standee' windows which became a feature of American city buses. This vehicle made use of hydraulic power for steering, brakes and door operation. In addition it had numerous safety features including brake application with a door open. *Below*

Leyland and AEC examples of underfloor-engined vehicles with front-entrance and flat floor, scarcely distinguishable without their maker's badge.

the engine not mounted in the conventional position at the front. The engine was mounted in a transverse position at the rear, blocking the site of the traditional rear passenger platform for double-deckers. Production of Atlanteans began in 1958 and Daimler Fleetlines in 1960. Midland Red adopted this last make of vehicle instead of continuing with their own design of double-decker. The Fleetlines were normally supplied with Gardner engines.

Transmissions by this time were very sophisticated. Daimler vehicles had fluid flywheels and preselective gearboxes and AEC also had this arrangement. Leyland had a synchro mesh gearbox, but these gave way to semi-automatic and fully-automatic epicyclic gearboxes and this arrangement was fitted to Atlanteans and Fleetlines. The change to rear-engined double-deckers as a standard then began. Considerable impetus was given to this design when one-man operation was permitted on double-deckers.

Bristol produced the VRL in 1966 which was a third rear-engined double-decker, but the engine was mounted to the off side corner and not centrally in the transverse position. The VRL, too, was one of the first 10 m (33 ft) long double-deckers, although subsequently Atlanteans and Fleetlines were built to this size, in fact some designs were made 11 m

The DMS type came to London in 1971 as a one-man operated double-decker, based originally on the Daimler Fleetline. Subsequently after Daimler commercial vehicles became absorbed by the Leyland organization the vehicles were based on the Leyland B20 chassis with Park Royal or Metro-Cammell-Weymann bodywork, 44 seats upstairs and 24 down with provision for a further 21 standing. The overall length was only 9·3 m (30½ ft) but the width was now 2·5 m (8ft 2½ in).

The Leyland Titan which is difficult to distinguish from the MCW and both of which are now being produced in quantity. It is the successor to the Atlantean and is built alongside the Leyland National at the Workington factory.

(36 ft) long. Double-deckers could have been made longer but weight restrictions made it prudent not to stretch the vehicles to the maximum the law permitted in size because double-decker buses could now be built to seat 86 passengers comfortably. More powerful engines were required and to keep the weight down the practice of turbo charging smaller engines came into vogue.

By 1970 the Leyland organization had almost obtained a monopoly of bus manufacture, having taken over the production of the Daimler Fleetline. Other manufacturers, especially foreign competitors, tried to challenge this monopoly. Volvo produced the Ailsa in Scotland, using a turbo-charged engine placed in the conventional position, the vehicle was in fact of semi-integral construction and appeared in 1973. A further challenge was made, also in 1973, by the collaboration of the Scania-Vabis organization with Metro-Cammell to produce the Metro-Scania, This has led the MCW organization to produce their own Metropolitan as a direct competitor to the new Leyland Titan and these two buses will probably be the new double-deckers in London for the next decade.

A 1979 Metrobus for the West Midlands PTE with Metro-Cammell 73-seat body and Gardner 6-cylinder engine. It has a body length of 10 m (33 ft).

Metro-Scania buses began with the running units being worked
from Sweden to England as a chassis frame. The frame was then
split at Birmingham and the integral double-decker or single-decker
constructed on the sub assemblies. This shows a left-hand drive
unit before being divided after delivery from Sweden.

Vehicle manufacture in Britain

In 1926 there were at least 30 makes of chassis suitable for buses being manufactured in Britain and there were a further 12 from America and at least another 12 from the Continent of Europe. In addition, of course, there were separate bodybuilders and over 60 of these provided bus and coach bodies on any of these chassis, according to the requirements of the customer. By 1969 there were only 5 manufacturers whose marques appeared on buses and coaches, although Leyland at this time was continuing to use some of the names of organizations which they had already absorbed.

The Leyland Bus and Truck Division, whose antecedents go back to 1896, became Leyland Motors Ltd. in 1907. After World War I they were among the leading builders of chassis and engines for passenger-carrying vehicles and by 1969, through acquisition and amalgamation, they had achieved a dominant, almost monopoly, position in Britain in this field. In 1951 Leyland obtained control of Albion Motors Ltd., the leading Scottish chassis manufacturer and in 1962 merged with Associated Commercial Vehicles Ltd., the successors to AEC, the 'Builders of London's Buses'. AEC had previously acquired Maudslay and Crossley and also two leading bodybuilders, Park Royal Vehicles Ltd. and Charles H. Roe Ltd. An amalgamation with the British Motor Corporation in 1969 brought both Guy and Daimler into the Leyland orbit.

Subsequently, after the National Bus Company was formed in 1969, management control of Bristol Commercial Vehicles and the Eastern Coach Works Ltd. was transferred to Leyland and in consequence a new company Leyland National was formed to manufacture a standard bus. After nationalization in 1948 Bristol and Eastern Coach Works had been permitted only to manufacture for nationalized organizations and not to sell their new vehicles on the open market.

By 1940 two basic forms of double-decker had evolved, the highbridge with a height of 4·42 m (14½ ft) and the lowbridge 4·12 m (13½ ft), the latter for use on routes with restricted height due to low bridges, trees or other obstructions. The highbridge type had a conventional seating arrangement, with a centre gangway on the top deck, while the lowbridge type had a sunken side gangway with seats for 4 altogether in rows on the top deck, which made the conductor's task difficult when collecting fares.

In 1949 Bristol produced a low height design which was christened the 'Lodekka'. This vehicle

A Bristol with low height body and conventional rear platform by Eastern Coach Works in the fleet of United Automobile Services.

A 1947 AEC Regent III with Park Royal bodywork for Birmingham Corporation, now part of the West Midlands PTE. The design and appearance is quite different from the contemporary vehicles on virtually the same chassis for London Transport.

allowed a normal seating layout with a centre gangway on the top deck, but within the same overall height of the lowbridge type. The design incorporated a split propellor shaft driving either side of a dropped centre rear axle, enabling a sunken floor to be provided in the lower saloon, thereby eliminating any step between the rear platform and the lower saloon. The first prototype of this bus appeared in 1949. Later the Lodekka design incorporated a 9·14 m × 2·44 m (30 ft × 8 ft) body. Over 5,000 buses of this basic design were built, going into operation with the nationalized companies.

In order that the advantage of this design could be obtained by other operators, manufacturing rights to the basic patents were acquired by Dennis who, between 1958 and 1967, produced the 'Loline' bus which sold on the open market. In 1969, however, Bristol became part of the Leyland organization and once more were permitted to sell buses of their design to any operator. The Lodekka can be classed among the 'greats' of bus design, holding a strong place in the bus field for at least fifteen years, but by the time it became available on the open market, the design was outdated.

Two other manufacturers (although not builders of double-deckers) remained outside the Leyland orbit and both are connected with American multi-

A strong export market was built up for the small Bedford. This is a unit operating in Buenos Aires typical of the type used in this city. Most services are operated by syndicates and associations with small vehicles, many of which have doors on both sides because in the many one-way streets stops are provided on both sides of the street.

A Plaxton Supreme body on a Ford chassis typical of the modern private hire and touring coach of 1978.

national companies. Vauxhall Motors of Luton had become part of the General Motors Corporation in 1931 when they produced their first commercial vehicle in England to replace the Chevrolet which had been imported. The vehicles were given the name Bedford and were small 14 and 20 seaters. By 1934 it was claimed that almost half the buses in Britain which were only capable of carrying 20 people were Bedfords and many vehicles have been produced for export. The British Ford Motor Company of Dagenham produced a specialized chassis, particularly for PSV (public service vehicle)

A specialized body was provided for the vehicles operated to the requirements of the Dartford Tunnel Authority in order to convey bicycles through the tunnel. The vehicles were built on Ford Thames Commercial chassis in 1963 and were 9·14 m (30 ft) long. They seated 30 passengers and carried 30 bicycles but the traffic was poor and the service ceased in 1965.

A large number of Leyland Nationals have been purchased by London Transport and given the type letter LS. The first one entered service in 1973, 10·3 m (just under 34 ft) long and 2·5 m (8 ft 2½ in) wide, with seating for 36 with a further 29 standing and suitable for one-man operation.

duty, called the Thames until 1965, when the name Ford was again used.

In 1969 there was the new development of a bus jointly produced by British Leyland and the National Bus Company from a new factory established at Workington, this was the Leyland National. The first appeared late in 1970. There were two basic models, one 10·3 m (33 ft 11 in) with a laden weight of just over 13 tons, seating 36 and the other was a longer version 11·3 m (37 ft 2 in) long seating 52.

One of the distinctive features of this new bus is the raised roof at the rear which contains ventilating and heating equipment. The engine used is small but turbo-charged and mounted horizontally at the rear under the floor driving through a fluid coupling a pneumocyclic gearbox. The main body which is of integral construction is provided with air suspension, being built of specific nodules so that access doors and emergency exits can be varied to meet individual operator's requirements or particular country's vehicle regulations. The long version with a two door layout would have the passenger capacity reduced from 52 to 48. The shorter version supplied to London Transport had the standard seating. It was felt during the planning of this vehicle that it would replace many double-deckers in Britain and, at the same time, be a very suitable bus for export.

Construction and use regulations

Before 1925 buses and coaches were no more than specialized bodies placed on truck or elongated car chassis. Certain chassis were specifically designed for bus work, but the London General B type, for example, subsequently the Bristol and the Midland S.O.S., were, at first, basically lorry type chassis on to which bodies were built, usually by specialist bodybuilders and not by the chassis manufacturer.

Various licensing authorities set their own standards for the size of vehicles. The Metropolitan Police and the Edinburgh City Magistrates were two organizations that had a profound effect on the design of buses at the time.

London restricted bodywork to a maximum length of 7·62 m (25 ft) and width of 2·18 m (7 ft 2 in) and also had a restrictive turning circle. In addition, covered tops to double-deckers or the protection of drivers by glass-fronted screens were not permitted until well after these amenities were being provided elsewhere. It was late in 1925 before the Metropolitan Police agreed to covered tops and March 1928 before approval was given to pneumatic tyres.

By 1926 the pneumatic tyre had progressed to the extent that all single-deckers could be fitted with pneumatic tyres, but difficulties still existed when

The BMMO (Midland Red) type C5 underfloor-engined 37-seater coach with a forward-entrance. It was built in the company's own workshop in Carlyle Road Birmingham in 1959 for operation over the M1 Motorway then just completed. This was the successor to a long line of underfloor-engined buses developed by Midland Red.

An 'NS' type with a special form of domed covered top to enable the bus to operate through the Blackwall Tunnel, but notice that in 1927 it still has no pneumatic tyres.

applied to double-deckers. Two-axle double-deckers were limited to a maximum of 7·62 m (25 ft) but 3-axle double-deckers could be made up to 9·14 m (30 ft) which spread the load over more wheels and pneumatic tyres were within reach.

In the 1930 Road Traffic Act (among other matters) a 4-wheeled double-decker was permitted to be 7·93 m (26 ft) long and this length remained the regulation until June 1950 when the 4-wheeled double-decker could be stretched to 8·23 m (27 ft). At the same time the single-decker on 4 wheels was extended from 8·38 m to 9·14 m (27½ ft to 30 ft). These increases in length were achieved at the same time as a 2·44 m (8 ft) wide bus was accepted as the standard. The width of the bus had been restricted generally to 2·29 m (7½ ft) until World War II when some wider buses, intended for export, were allowed to operate in England. The Ministry of Transport was then petitioned to allow these vehicles to continue and, despite some reluctance, from 1 July 1946 2·44 m (8 ft) wide bus and trolleybus routes could be operated with the permission of the Traffic Commissioners.

Buses 2·44 m (8 ft) wide commenced running in London from 14 May 1949 but only on specified routes. In 1950 special road tests were put in hand to prove that buses of the width could operate through

A 1950 Crossley, with Crossley bodywork, for Birmingham
Corporation, with 54 seats and conventional rear open platform.

the centre of the city without restriction and this was achieved in time for the Routemaster, the new London standard bus being developed in the 1950s as a 2·44 m (8 ft) wide vehicle. The first prototype Routemaster went into service in London on 8 February 1955. This bus seated 64 passengers and the design was a joint development specifically for London conditions by London Transport, AEC and Park Royal Vehicles. In 1979 these buses were still providing the backbone service in London and because of their continued reliability were destined to last another ten years. A 35-year maximum life for a bus without a major rebuild is unique and justifies the first high initial cost which was severely criticized when the type was first introduced.

From 1 July 1956 the regulations were again changed to permit 2-axle double-deckers to be constructed 9·14 m (30 ft) long with the maximum gross weight to be increased by 2 tons to 14 tons. This change in regulation had the effect of producing a longer version of the Routemaster which became the RML. The fundamental design of the bus remained unchanged but an additional bay was built into the central section of the body. Then in 1961 a further amendment permitted single-decker buses to be built 11 m (36 ft) long. This paved the way for the construction of high capacity single-deckers and

it was thought that double-deckers would become unnecessary although the regulations allowed them to be built up to 11 m (36 ft) long and 2·5 m (8 ft 2½ in) wide as well. Builders, however, did not take advantage of this size relaxation because it was found difficult to keep within the total weight limitation. By 1962 buses 2·29 m (7½ ft) wide were no longer being built.

The main gross weight limit was raised a further 2 tons to 16 tons in 1961, passenger weight usually being calculated at 16 passengers to the ton. An 11 m (36 ft) Leyland Atlantean, for example, theoretically could now be built to carry 100 passengers, but such a vehicle would, without doubt, exceed the maximum gross weight.

One of the problems of this continual change in the regulations is that it has complicated rather than simplified bus construction. Double-decker buses could now be provided at lengths from 8·23-11 m (27-36 ft) with entrances either forward of or behind the front wheels, or with double doorways and stairways, either directly behind the driver or further down the vehicle, whereas previously with only a rear platform double-decker of limited length, a standard format had been achieved which had lasted (with only minor modifications necessary) for at least two decades.

A special fleet of 65 vehicles were built 9·14 m (30 ft) long and 2·44 m (8 ft) wide with a 1½-deck type body to provide a luggage compartment for airport traffic being operated for several years by London Transport on behalf of British European Airways between South Kensington terminal and London airport. The basis of this vehicle was the AEC Regal Mark IV. The underfloor-engined coach had a body built by Park Royal with 37 seats.

The RTW type for London Transport was the first 2·44 m (8 ft) wide bus to operate in London, although still within a length of 8 m (26 ft). They began working in 1949. These vehicles had Leyland engines but AEC fluid flywheel and preselective gearbox.

The photograph above shows the RM, or Routemaster, which began bulk operation in 1959. Right is the RML which was produced in 1961 with an extra 71 cm (2 ft 4 in) in bodywork length which raised the seating capacity from 64 to 72.

Because of legal restrictions public service vehicles in Britain were not worked by one person, except small vehicles (seating 14 or less) in very special circumstances. Flat fares which were almost universal on urban services in North America from the horse tram era encouraged the adoption of one-man operation from an early date, but in Britain it was considered an unsafe practice for the driver to have to be concerned with complicated fare collection as well as driving the vehicle. Subsequently the regulations raised the limit to a passenger capacity not greater than 20.

With a flat fare system, of course, the fare collection can be simplified by the use of automatic registers, dispensing with the need to provide tickets as long as the passenger is compelled to pass the driver either at the start of his journey or at its termination. Both methods are in use, depending on the route.

In 1952 Huddersfield was given permission to operate one route as a one-man operated route

The Leyland Atlantean was in general production from 1958 to 1967. Some were constructed by Albion with Alexander bodywork for Glasgow Corporation and LA284 in the fleet 9·14 m (30 ft) long and 2·44 m (8 ft) wide was exhibited at the Munich International Transport Exhibition in 1965.

An AEC long Regent with 70-seater bodywork and front-entrance by Weymann in 1958 for a South Wales operation in the BET group.

A conventional highbridge double-decker for Southdown in 1956 on a Guy Arab chassis but provided with rear platform doors on an 8·23 m (27 ft) length.

A General Motors 45-seater New York bus in 1951. The 'standee' windows were provided for the benefit of the large number of standing passengers that were permitted.

under 'Defence Regulations' using 43-seater vehicles. The law by this time permitted 26-seater one-man operated vehicles, but under the Defence Regulations the Traffic Commissioners could authorize larger vehicles under special circumstances. Flat fares were not in operation and special ticket and coin changing racks were provided to facilitate the issuing of different denomination tickets and provide change.

One-man operation with buses larger than 26-seaters began in the Central London Area on 18 November 1964 with RF type 39-seaters which were fitted with power-operated doors, with the fare being paid on entrance. At this time the fares varied and change was given. One-man experiments had been tried with various vehicles and differing methods of collecting and issuing fares over the previous ten years to find the ideal arrangement, not only in London but by provincial operators as well, and there were as many solutions as there were problems.

In 1966 a further venture in this direction appeared in London with 11 m (36 ft) long and 2·5 m (8 ft 2½ in) wide vehicles, seating a maximum of 46 passengers. These buses had front-entrances and centre-exits after the American style, with power-operated doors. Some of these buses were used on one-man

The Red Arrow 'standee' bus with capacity for 73 passengers with only 25 seated appeared on special London Transport routes in April 1966. The body, constructed by MCW, utilized an AEC horizontal diesel motor and was designed for one-man operation at a flat fare.

The Guy Wulfrunian double-decker first appeared in 1959 and was an advanced design with a front engine but arranged to take a long body 9·14 m (30 ft) long by 2·44 m (8 ft) wide. Unusually, the stairway was placed on the near side and straight up, not in the conventional position behind the driver. The bus was also provided with disc brakes, air suspension and low unladen weight, within an overall height of 4·12 m (13½ ft). Only a limited number were built and production ceased in 1965.

The RF type was placed in service with London Transport in 1951. A fleet of over 700 with MCW bodies on AEC Regal chassis were operated with a number of body variations but all with front-entrance which enabled them to be converted for one-man operation with 39 seats in 1964.

routes while others were fitted with a special interior with only 25 seats at the rear and the front area between the doorways available for standing.

In the late 1960s all operators were suffering from full employment which made recruitment difficult, so that the Ministry of Transport looked favourably on increasing the capacity of one-man operated buses for more than 26 passengers and consequently between 1966 and 1968 most operators converted many single-decker routes to one-man operation by modifying existing front-entrance vehicles. Agreement was subsequently obtained for one-man operation of double-deckers and by 1968 these were beginning to be operated, some with only a front-entrance, but others with a centre-exit as well. The agreement that one-man operation could be applied to double-deckers resurrected the demand for such vehicles which since the introduction of the large capacity single-decker had gone into a decline. However, on very busy urban routes with frequent passenger exchange it was still found desirable to operate two-man double-deckers because otherwise stopping delays become excessive. It is this situation which has extended the life of the RM type in London, since it is impossible to operate some routes efficiently on a one-man basis with the existing fare system.

A Birmingham Corporation bus (now West Midlands) undergoing the tilt test which is compulsory for all double-deckers. The base platform has been tilted 30° and the bus list has become 38½° but still remains stable.

Bus organization in Britain

All the bus and tramway operating concerns, both municipal and private, within a prescribed area surrounding London amalgamated in 1933 to form London Transport and became the largest single operating concern in Britain with a fleet of over 6,000 buses. Prior to 1933 the largest bus operator had been the London General Omnibus Co., and almost from the beginning of mechanical traction there had been an associated manufacturing concern which in 1912 became the Associated Equipment Company with the marque AEC. In 1933 this concern became independent, selling buses all over the world but continued to build most of London's buses in collaboration with London Transport until 1968 when it became part of the Leyland Truck and Bus Division and subsequently the AEC marque disappeared.

Perhaps the optimum design of the now old fashioned conventional double-decker, with a chassis and separate bodywork with a rear-entrance open platform for operation by two men, was the RT designed for London Transport requirements and built by AEC. This was one of the most successful bus designs ever built being first produced before World War II and over 4,800 of this type were provided with bodies by a number of bodybuilders

Until 1973 David MacBrayne was the most important name in transport in the Scottish Highlands and had been for almost a century. Shown is an AEC Regal III with 35-seater bodywork by Roe of Leeds making use of the extra length to 9·14 m (30 ft) in 1953.

An AEC RT with Weymann body soon after delivery to London Transport before the main advert panels had been fixed.

for operation in London. Leyland subsequently built vehicles to a similar design of which 500 were the first in London to be 2·44 m (8 ft) wide. 1979 saw the last vehicle of this type operating on the streets of London.

The largest operating group, however, is the National Bus Company which has developed from the Transport Act of 1947, the 'Nationalization Act' which encouraged public ownership of all the basic means of public transport. 1950 was the year when public transport was used by the British public to its maximum. The following years saw a slow decline in the number of people carried on public transport mainly arising from a number of unrelated things, the principal of these being the growth in the ownership of private cars, the advance of television and the improvement in cold storage for foods, making it unnecessary for the housewife to shop every day. The number of buses in operation in the early 1950s reached some 75,000 vehicles and is still of this order today.

Thomas Tilling Ltd. who had interests in about half the large operating companies in England, sold their bus interests in 1948 to the newly formed British Transport Commission which then gave them control of about 14,000 of the above 75,000. However, it also gave them a share in the control of a further 11,000 buses which had been jointly owned with the British Electric Traction Co. This concern was against nationalization at that time and would not sell its share of the bus business to the BTC. The 1947 Act contemplated permissive 'area schemes' under some form of Regional Boards, but this machinery of acquisition was not proceeded with, so that the 'status quo' of part nationalization and part 'private enterprise' continued until 1968 when the British Electric Traction Co. decided to sell its bus interests to the Transport Holding Company which had been formed by the Transport Act in 1962 to hold the shares of all nationally owned bus undertakings. At the time this included the Thomas Tilling group, the Red and White group and the Scottish Motor Traction group.

In the Transport Act of 1968 the National Bus Company was set up to be the bus operating authority in England and Wales controlling some 18,000 buses. Its operating area excluded Scotland which was separately organized as the Scottish Omnibuses Ltd. controlling another 6,000 buses. The National Bus Co., is responsible to the Ministry of Transport while Scottish Omnibuses is responsible to the Secretary of State for Scotland. Under this scheme some rationalization of the operating companies took place and some familiar fleet names disappeared. However, many of the traditional names remained, such as United, Northern General, Ribble, Eastern National, Western National, Southdown, East Kent, Crosville and Western Welsh.

The long-distance routes that crossed company territorial boundaries were now worked under the fleet name 'National' with the management company shown in very small letters. Local services continued to have the more conventional fleet

Ribble Motor Services Ltd., a concern with roots going back to 1919, grew to be one of the largest companies in the British Electric Traction Organization. This vehicle is a 61-seater Leyland with Burlingham bodywork including a patent sliding door on the rear platform.

Nationalization has brought about standardization not only of vehicles but of liveries as well. A Leyland Leopard with Duple bodywork seems to owe allegiance to two operating companies and is shown in the white livery of National Travel which first appeared in 1972.

An SMT Leyland TD5 of 1938 with Leyland lowbridge bodywork seating 27 upstairs and 26 down. The SMT subsequently became Eastern Scottish, in the 1968 re-organization.

Another TD5 originally built with lowbridge bodywork in 1940 before production ceased because of the war. In 1950 the chassis was re-bodied by Park Royal with a highbridge and seating for 2 more making 54 in all, for operation by Southdown, a company which began in 1915 eventually becoming part of the British Automobile Traction empire until 1968.

names on the operating buses, but the distinctive livery began to disappear so that the separate companies tended to lose some of their individuality. Subsequently the coaching and long-distance ser-vices were transferred to a new operating company National Travel (NBC) Ltd. to co-ordinate the long-distance and coaching activities of the area companies and their touring subsidiaries. The actual operations were transferred to five area National Travel Companies and the individual names which had been familiar for decades began to disappear for such mundane names as National Travel linked to various points of the compass.

The National Bus Company also took over the Railway Board's interest in joint undertakings with municipal authorities, in particular those at Halifax, Huddersfield and Sheffield and these names subsequently disappeared into Passenger Transport Executives, or PTEs.

In 1969 there were 92 municipal bus operating authorities ranging from Glasgow, Manchester and Birmingham with over 1,200 buses each to Ramsbottom with only 12. By 1979 43 of these authorities had vanished, leaving only 49 still controlled by municipal authorities, and responsible for a total of about 6,000 buses. Of these 49, 37 were in England, 9 in Wales and 3 in Scotland. The largest in Scotland, at present, being the undertaking known as Lothian incorporating the services previously covered by Edinburgh Corporation and responsible for some 600 vehicles. The largest in England is Nottingham with 400 buses. However, there are a number with fleets as small as 50, such as Fylde, previously named Lytham St. Anne's and East Staffordshire, previously Burton-on-Trent.

Most of the large municipal authorities have disappeared into Passenger Transport Executives which were created by means of the Transport Act of 1968. West Midlands was the first to be formed and began operating 1 October 1969, acquiring Birmingham with 1,400 vehicles, Walsall having 268, West Bromwich with 120 and Wolverhampton with 280. Birmingham previously had owned the largest municipal fleet in Britain. Later, in 1974, Coventry with 308 vehicles was taken over.

As from 3 December 1973 the West Midlands Passenger Transport Authority took over the bus services of the Midland Red which were within the West Midlands Metropolitan County to enable all stage carriage services in the county to be controlled by the PTE. This takeover included 400 vehicles and 1,500 staff, together with six Midland Red garages. This considerably reduced Midland Red, previously the largest bus operating unit outside London, but in turn helped to ensure that the West Midlands PTE became the largest bus operator outside London.

Merseyside, incorporating Liverpool, Birkenhead and Wallasey, began operating 1 December 1969. Subsequently, in 1974, Southport and St. Helens were included. Tyneside began operating 1 January 1970, including Newcastle-upon-Tyne and South Shields, and Sunderland was added on 1 April 1973.

An MCW Metropolitan in the fleet of London Transport.

The South East Lancashire North East Cheshire Authority which immediately became known as Selnec was the second PTE to go into operation, taking over 11 municipal authorities, ranging from Manchester with 1,250 vehicles to Ramsbottom with only 12. Operation began 1 November 1969. In 1974 the name of the organization was simplified to Greater Manchester PTE adding Wigan to the original 11.

Greater Glasgow PTE (now called Strathclyde) took over the Glasgow Corporation fleet of 1,318 vehicles and began operating on 1 June 1973. In 1974 West Yorkshire PTE became responsible for Bradford, Halifax, Huddersfield and Leeds, while South Yorkshire took on Doncaster, Rotherham and Sheffield.

The Passenger Transport Executives are not only responsible for operating bus services on their own account, but hire or subsidize services operated by the National Bus Company or other operators. In Scotland, of course, the largest operator is the Scottish Bus Group which controls a number of operating concerns.

Under the 1968 Act, London Transport was required to reduce its operating area to that which was covered by the Greater London Council so the Country Area section became London Country Bus Company and part of the National Bus organization.

After 1969 the Green Line was no longer a London Transport operating responsibility and took on the look of the National Bus Company receiving an allocation of the coaches then being built. Shown is a 1979 AEC Reliance with Duple Dominant bodywork, seating 49 passengers and with space for luggage for airport service.

In Scotland a Scottish Transport Group was set up in 1969 to integrate all State owned transport organizations. This organization then controlled Scottish Bus Group of Companies, David MacBrayne with shipping interests as well as bus services, and the Caledonian Steam Packet Company which had been the railways-managed shipping company. The result of this was a consolidation of interests. The shipping organization became Cal-Mac, joining the interests of the Caledonian Steam Packet Co., and Mac-Brayne together, while MacBrayne bus interests were transferred to the Scottish Bus Group and the name which had been synonymous with the Scottish Highlands for almost a century disappeared from the side of buses.

One of the interesting features of this legislation was that from 1 January 1969 the grant paid to public service vehicle operators to offset the heavy fuel tax was increased from 4p to 8p (10d to 1/7d) per gallon. This was in addition to the bus grants covering the purchase of new buses. Fuel tax was first introduced in 1909 at ½p (1½d) per gallon on petrol. In 1915 the tax was raised to 1.25p (3d) and by 1938 it had reached 3.75p (9d) per gallon. Governments continued to add fuel taxes, but tried to cushion these imposts from the providers of public transport by giving rebates of various kinds.

A Guy Arab of 1955 in the fleet of Western SMT, part of the Scottish Bus Group. The Alexander bodywork seated 30 passengers. The bus was withdrawn in 1969.

An example of a dual-purpose vehicle on an Albion chassis operating on a local town service but available for coach touring.

In addition to the National Bus Company, London Transport, the seven Passenger Transport Executives and the 49 municipal operators, there are still a large number of private operators—not many in the stage carriage business because this type of operation is not profitable without some sort of subsidization—but coach services, holiday excursions, tours and private hire work is generally in the hands of private operators, mostly owning less than ten vehicles. However, there are a number of large operators with considerable fleets, such as Grey Green, the London-based coach proprietors and long-distance bus operator, and Wallace Arnold with tours organized from points as far apart as Leeds and Torquay. There are probably as many as 5,000 separate operators in this particular group in the United Kingdom.

Due to the reduction in the country bus services in sparsely populated districts, the Post Office had to increase the operation of mail vans. It was a short step to introduce Post Buses which carried passengers as well, subsidized by their duty as a Post Van. After some experimental services, both in Wales and Scotland, a Post Bus system began to be set up in remote areas from 1968, especially in Scotland. Minibus-type vehicles are used, seating less than 14 passengers.

Excursions and tours

In the nineteenth century day excursions to places of interest were arranged by means of horse-drawn vehicles with rows of bench seats facing forward. Sometimes the floor of the 'carriage' was sloped upwards to the rear so that the passengers could obtain a better view. Motorization of this type of vehicle began in 1904 and the name charabanc (derived from the French for 'carriage with benches') survived for a particular type of body with cross seating. By 1914 extended tours lasting up to a week or more using such vehicles had begun to be fairly common from industrial centres such as Wolverhampton and Liverpool to the beautiful countryside nearby.

Charabancs tended to be lighter than their contemporary buses and were fitted with pneumatic tyres from about 1920. This was in fact used as an advertising gimmick in 1925 to notify potential customers that excursions were being made with vehicles on pneumatic tyres.

By 1919 every holiday resort in Britain had a line of charabancs plying for hire on day excursions to local places of interest, and it was about 1930 before this type of vehicle gave way to the enclosed motor coach on these stands.

About 1927 long-distance bus routes began to be introduced which called for vehicles which were faster, more reliable and much more comfortable. The coachbuilders of the day responded to these requirements and the vehicles that they subsequently produced were also in great demand for excursions and tour work.

Some operators had tried to obtain vehicles which they could use for excursion work or for regular bus work, so that the seating was arranged in bus format with a so-called sunshine roof provided which could be rolled back.

The opening of the first motorway in Britain in 1958 led to a new development for express motor coaches, the high-speed vehicle capable of operating up to the permitted motorway limit which for buses and coaches was 48 km/h (30 mph) at that time. The Midland Red concern was the first to take advantage of the relaxation that the motorway provided, producing a 37-seater vehicle with a turbocharged 8 litre underfloor engine.

Coaches for tours, excursions and regular express services continue to be a high proportion of the buses operated in Britain. The two coachbuilders who dominate this market are Duple and Plaxton and only the expert can now tell the products of their establishments apart.

An early type of charabanc used before World War I. This type of
vehicle was easily converted to lorry or coal cart by a change of body
and some vehicles of this type were fitted with bodies having a
sloping floor allowing rear passengers better visibility forward.

The Plaxton Panorama, which appeared in 1958, provided wide
windows with improved visibility for coaches used for touring. The
demand for such improvements was encouraged by the awards
established by the British Coach Rally, an annual event now passed
its 22nd year.

A typical 'torpedo' type charabanc constructed on a Karrier chassis about 1920. Each row of seats was normally provided with its own hinged 'door', often only on the near side, some passengers were accommodated beside the driver. Most commercial vehicle builders at this time provided chassis to which charabanc bodies could be fitted. The body was usually fitted with a 'Cape Cart Hood' for inclement weather, including canvas side screens with mica look-outs.

The Scottish Motor Traction operated excursions and tours from Edinburgh before World War I with Lothian vehicles built in their own workshops. Vehicles of this type were among the first to have the driver beside the engine providing seats for 31 passengers—a very high capacity at this time.

A Bristol with Eastern Coachwork long-distance and touring body
with observation windows—a design which was very popular with
the large operating groups.

With the opening of the motorway Ribble introduced a new standard to coach travel by introducing Leyland Atlanteans with MCW bodywork with buffet and toilet on the lower deck and seats for 16, while 34 passengers were accommodated in the upper saloon. The 'Gay Hostess' vehicles were used on the principal trunk services from Lancashire to London by Ribble and associated companies. Each vehicle was capable of approximately 640 km (400 miles) operation per day. They were withdrawn in 1972 because the sophisticated provisions were unnecessary since conventional coaches could stop at motorway service stations.

Glenton Tours is now one of the few operators that specify a centre doorway. The Volvo provided with Plaxton coachwork in 1978 was modified to meet their requirements. This firm, established in 1928, renews the fleet regularly so that no coach in regular service is over 7 years old.

One of the first underfloor type coaches to be operated in London. A Leyland Royal Tiger in the fleet of Grey Green Coaches. In 1950, this coach with a body 9·14 m (30 ft) long and 2·44 m (8 ft) wide, seated 41 passengers and had a central-entrance doorway which was very popular with many operators for several years. The coachwork on this vehicle is by Harrington of Brighton — now no longer in the coachbuilding business.

Continental practice

There is no common practice on the continent of Europe, even within the EEC, which means that there are considerable differences both in the vehicles and the methods of operation in the various countries of Europe.

The operations in West Germany are dominated by two large operators, the Deutsche Bundesbahn (The German Federal Railways) and the Deutsche Bundespost (The Post Office), both of whose operations have a long history. The various railways began bus operation to feed their systems, while the post office began to carry passengers on the vehicles carrying the mail, some of these services stretching back to horse-bus operation. The first motor bus service in Bavaria was operated by a Daimler post bus in 1906. Between them these two concerns operate over 10,000 vehicles in West Germany, out of a total of 58,000 vehicles, the rest being operated by some 5,000 separate undertakings.

After the end of World War II the tramway networks were in a devastated state and repairs took a long time, so buses that could tow trailers became a regular practice of German operation and this continued until the 1960s when the Government decreed that the haulage of passenger trailers was

A Büssing with trailer in the fleet of the German Post Office.

A Büssing of articulated form in the service of a Dutch area company.

A 1915 Berlin double-decker, seating 42 passengers — 6 people were permitted to stand on the rear platform. The vehicle was narrow at 2·18 m (7 ft 2 in) width.

A modern double-decker for Berlin 2·5 m (8 ft 2 in) wide and over 11 m (36 ft) long. The headroom in the top saloon is only 1·7 m (5 ft 8 in) and the overall height of the vehicle is 4 m (13 ft).

to be discontinued. The long established commercial vehicle builder, MAN, then produced the articulated bus, with Büssing following with a similar design. This enabled operators of routes which had used a bus plus trailer to continue to provide large capacity vehicles and manning levels were reduced because for a number of years where trailers were used two conductors, one for each vehicle, had been provided. Some 2,000 articulated buses are now operating in West Germany of which only about 100 are operated by the two big concerns. The articulated buses are mostly operated by the municipal authorities which make up nearly 200 different operators.

A 1½-deck Büssing in the service of a German interurban operator. Several manufacturers produced buses of this type.

There are very few double-deckers operated in West Germany, the largest fleet being that in West Berlin, an urban bus service first started in Berlin in 1905. ABOAG (the operating authority at the time), like many other early motor bus concerns, found it necessary to build its own vehicles designing an open-top double-decker in 1913 which set the pattern for Berlin vehicles until 1925, although World War I interrupted their development. Top covers were fitted from about this time and Berlin remained faithful to double-deckers.

The 1967 Berlin double-deckers had Büssing underfloor diesel engines with Voith transmission, air suspension and power-assisted steering, construction being integral the vehicles were assembled by bodybuilders, one of the main contractors being Orenstein & Koppel. The buses work on the one-man principle because the fare structure in Berlin is now flat fare.

Another design of vehicle popular in Germany is the 1½ deck vehicle used by a number of interurban operators.

One of the largest bus and coach builders in West Germany is Kässbohrer of Ulm, the builders of the Setra marque of vehicles, the letters standing in German for 'self supporting'. This concern actually designed the Continental Trailways 'Golden Eagle'

A Mercedes in Sao Paulo, South America. Most buses in this city operate with front-entrance and rear-exit but passengers have to pass through a turnstile inside the bus.

A Schneider prototype bus of about 1909, for Paris. The seating capacity was 28, 12 in the first class and 9 in the second class, with a further 7 permitted to stand at the rear. Similar buses were provided by De Dion Bouton, and Renault.

transcontinental bus for the American market in 1955. The German marque that has world-wide fame, of course, is the Mercedes and this is now being built in factories outside Europe, especially South America and India.

In 1969 the German municipal authorities got together to obtain a standard design of urban bus. It was named after the municipal association, the Verband Offentlicher Verkehrsbetriebe, becoming the VOV design. Each chassis maker, Mercedes, Magirus-Deutz, Setra and MAN, provide their own components, but the general design is of a standard form. However, a number of dimensional changes have been allowed to suit particular operators although a standard length of 11 m (36 ft) was originally specified.

Italy also developed a standard urban bus from designs formulated by an operators' association—the main builder was Fiat. The bus was constructed on 11 and 12 m (36 and 39 ft) long designs, the longer version having more doorways, and was not of integral design, being a body built on a low chassis.

There have been two very big names in the French motor industry, Louis Renault and Marcus Berliet, the latter began manufacturing cars in 1896 subsequently entering the commercial vehicle field and became part of the Citroen organization in 1967. André Citroen started production of his first cars in 1919 and later built up the Citroen empire. Renault began producing commercial vehicles in 1906. Before 1928 the 'coal-scuttle' type front was typical of Renault vehicles, usually covering a 4-cylinder engine.

In 1955 the Société Anonyme des Véhicules Industriels et d'Equipement Méchanique was formed by amalgamating the Renault truck and bus division with Latil, Somua, Isobloc and Floirat organizations thus producing the marque now known as Saviem. In 1959 the bus manufacturing division of Chausson was also acquired, giving this group an overwhelming control of bus manufacturing in France equivalent to Leyland in Britain, General Motors in America, Fiat in Italy and Mercedes in West Germany. The De Dion Bouton organization which in the early years had provided buses not only in Paris, but in London and New York, had disappeared by 1927.

In 1949 the Chausson integrated bus was being produced at the rate of about one per hour. The vehicle followed one basic design, a 45-seater single-decker with the entrance forward by the driver but the engine and transmission in the orthodox position. This bus was constructed on a

The rear platform became a traditional feature of the Paris bus but in 1950 a more conventional bus with a rear engine appeared and by 1963 the rear platform was disappearing. A number of modern underfloor-engined buses have now entered service restoring the rear open platform, both in Lyon and Paris.

rotating jig, one of the first buses to be constructed in this way outside America. Both the Renault and Citroen organizations became interested in bus operating concerns in the early 1930s in order to control the sale of their products. About 1932 Citroen began operating a network of routes in various parts of France by means of a subsidiary concern, Transports Citroen, while Renault began to acquire shareholding in area-operating concerns. The standard size of buses in France was 11 m (36 ft) long and 2·25 m (7 ft 5 in) wide.

In the mountainous countries of Switzerland and Austria different conditions apply. The backbone of public transport throughout these two countries is provided by the Federal Railway systems which are generally protected by law against competition so that trunk bus routes are conspicuous by their absence. However, there are many districts and mountain routes not reached by the railway and these are usually served by the Post Office.

In Switzerland the Post Office is the largest bus operator, owning more vehicles than practically all the other operators put together. Apart from the municipally owned fleets all public service operators have to be licensed by the Post Office so the services appear in three forms. First are those operated directly by the Post Office with their own vehicles

A Chausson in the fleet of Les Rapides de Bourgogne, one of the
French area companies. It is typical of the cross-country French bus
with roof rack and single door beside the driver.

A Citroen in the service of Transports Citroen — it also includes the typical roof rack.

An early Car Alpin of the Swiss Post Office, first introduced in 1920 by Saurer for some of the mail services across the Alps. A feature was the Cape Cart Hood and side screens with mica look-outs for inclement weather and the rear luggage rack, 16 passengers could be carried.

A modern FBW Alpen Wagen with luggage trailer — a typical arrangement for the routes across the Alpine passes.

and many such services have a long history dating from the horse stage coach across the mountain passes or up remote valleys. Second are those directly 'hired' from private operators by the Post Office, such concerns operate Post Office type vehicles painted in their own livery. Then there is a third concession where agreement to carry the mail is not essential to the operation of a service which would probably be provided in any case. A number of the privately-owned railways operate services of this kind as feeders to their railway operation. Trailers for both passengers or luggage are permitted in Switzerland and Austria. A number of articulated buses are now being operated on urban services following the adoption of this type of vehicle in Zurich in the 1950s.

In Holland the influence of British design is in evidence since both Leyland and AEC had agreements with local manufacturers. The operations are controlled by a number of municipal authorities, the principal of these being Amsterdam, Rotterdam and The Hague which have produced a joint specification for their urban bus, originally known as the 'Three Cities Bus'. The general bus operation is dominated by a series of area companies associated with the railway administration which now have adopted a common yellow livery. Some of these companies

The Swiss Post Office, the PTT, is the largest bus operator in
Switzerland not only working scenic mountain routes or into remote
valleys not reached by the railway, but urban services as well. This
is a Saurer vehicle with an urban type body with automatic doors but
the post horn symbol is clearly visible giving the vehicle right of way
on mountain roads.

A Leyland-Verheul in the service of a Dutch area operator
connected with the State Railways.

are the successors to the light railways now abandoned. Many of the buses operated by these concerns are Leylands.

In Belgium the Brossel organization utilized AEC components to provide the buses for the operating concerns. Again, the services are dominated by the municipalities and one large, Government subsidized, nationwide operator, the Vicinal (the Belgian Light Railway) developed from the network of light railways (both steam and electric) which was a feature of travel in the Low Countries for several decades.

In Scandinavia all the countries have their individuality. In Denmark the manufacture is dominated by DAB which has strong links with Leyland, although it has been responsible for individual designs for specific purposes. The largest municipality is Copenhagen which is now an all bus city and which has a fleet composed mainly of Volvo and DAB, although imported Leyland chassis once were the backbone of the operation.

A DAB articulated bus in the service of the Danish State Railways. The prototype appeared in 1947 and the vehicles were subsequently known as the 'Red Worms'. The power unit was based on the Leyland Tiger and had a length of over 16·76 m (55 ft) and could carry 83 people with 53 seated.

Sweden has a number of reasonable-sized bus operators outside the municipal authorities of Stockholm and Gothenburg, but the principal operator is the Swedish State Railway. The Swedish Post Office also became a bus operator in 1923 with small-capacity vehicles in remote areas. By 1959 about 150 coaches, some with combined lorry and bus bodies, were being operated. Two manufacturers now dominate the scene, Scania-Vabis and Volvo, both old established firms which have secured valuable export markets even in Britain, so that, generally speaking, their products follow the general trend in contemporary designs.

The special operating problems of Norway are caused by the deep indents into the land mass occasioned by the fjords, thus many of the bus concerns are also ferry operators. Although the Railway Administration does operate bus services, these do not hold a dominating position as in Sweden. The buses in Norway must be prepared to carry anything reasonable that is offered and on many services special racks to carry bicycles or skis are provided and prams can also be accommodated. Although some vehicles are manufactured in the country by Strommens with running units from Leyland and other manufacturers, the home market is not large enough to support such an industry.

A Volvo in the Swedish State Railway fleet on a Stockholm suburban service.

The Swedish State Railways are the largest bus operators in Sweden, not only to feed the railway system but to provide interurban services between villages. This is a Swedish built Scania-Vabis.

A Leyland bus in Norway carrying the bicycles.

Norwegian buses have to be common carriers since they are the only link between remote villages and city life.

American practice

Four distinct types of bus have developed in North America. For inter-city and touring operation a powerful type of vehicle, usually provided with air-conditioning, almost invariably with power steering and ample luggage space, has been developed from the large private car. The inter-city bus services themselves developed from small beginnings when large limousines were used which had extended chassis adapted to take as many passengers as possible. The first true inter-city bus was said to have been developed by Frank Fageol in 1920, the man who later organized the company named Twin Coach and pioneered other bus developments. There are now really only three builders of inter-city vehicles left in the market, although the development to the present stage has been achieved by the competition of many concerns—AFC-Brill, Beck, Fageol, White, Yellow Coach, Mack and Flxible, to mention only a few of the larger ones. By 1928 6-cylinder engined buses were being provided by these firms. All have ceased trading in the general bus market, probably because General Motors has almost cornered the business since most vehicles, whoever they are built by, are now powered by General Motors engines and transmission systems.

General Motors constructed the fleet of Scenicruisers in 1950 for the Greyhound organization but when these required replacements Greyhound began constructing the MC6 and MC7 vehicles in their own factory. The 6-wheeled MC6 was 2·59 m (8½ ft) wide although such a width was not acceptable to all States in America and MC7 had to be built to 2·44 m (8 ft) width only. The MC6 vehicles were restricted to those States agreeing to the wider bus.

The second and third types of bus in America are related and have similar appearances, those for suburban operation having only one doorway adjacent to the driver while the city or transit type have two and sometimes three doorways but is still based on the same basic body design.

The Fifth Avenue Coach Company of New York started with horse buses in 1885 and began operating motor buses in 1906 because a tramway could not be constructed along this famous avenue. In 1916 due to wartime difficulties in obtaining French De Dion chassis, the Fifth Avenue began building their own double-deck buses. They continued to build buses to meet their needs until 1925 when the construction part of their business was sold to Yellow Coach. Yellow Coach continued to manufacture commercial vehicles, especially buses, until 1943 when they became part of the General Motors

An AFC-Brill 41-seater inter-city type bus of 1951 with an underfloor
Hall-Scott petrol engine in the fleet of a railway bus subsidiary.

The Prevost Car Co., a Canadian coachbuilder, was established in 1924 and subsequently began constructing all-steel highway coaches. The prototype for the Prestige coach went into service in 1968 which then sold not only to Canadian operators but all over North America. Although the design incorporates 3 axles the rearmost axle is not driven and is only single-tyred. The driven axle is powered by a rear mounted General Motors V8 oil engine. The transmission is either through a manually controlled gearbox or fully-automatic system. A special feature of the Prevost design is the high panorama windows allowing better visibility than is normally found in American buses. This unit is in the service of the Montreal operator that has the airport concession.

Motor Coach Industries, established in Winnipeg, Canada, became part of the Greyhound organization in 1957 and another factory was established in North Dakota USA to build vehicles not only for Greyhound but for other operators. This concern now supplies about 40 per cent of the inter-city buses in North America but they are usually fitted with General Motors transmissions and 8-cylinder V engines placed at the rear but in line. MC7, MC8 and MC9 are all similar vehicles, 12·2 m (40 ft) long on 3 axles but with different body details — the MC7 first appeared in 1968 and the MC9, as shown, in 1977.

A New York double-decker, a type which ran on Fifth Avenue for many years, built at first by the Fifth Avenue Coach Co. themselves and then by Yellow Coach.

organization which eventually dominated the bus market. Over 80 per cent of the suburban and transit bus market (if the provision of engines is included) is now controlled by General Motors.

A rival left in the urban and suburban market is Flxible but they also fit General Motors units. The trade name was spelt without an 'e' for registration purposes. Flxible developed from a motor-cycle sidecar construction company and when motor cycles went out of fashion they began building bodies of all kinds, especially buses, of the extended limousine type.

Another builder is AM General which has developed from the wartime Kaiser organization which obtained contracts to make vehicles from other people's designs. In 1972 they began concentrating on making transit-type vehicles using transverse General Motors engines. This company also contracted to build the MAN articulated bus for operation in America in 1976.

In 1929, Fageol produced for the first time what was described as a twin-engined vehicle which then went into production for the next eight years. The Fageol brothers formed the Twin Coach Company to exploit this design with separate engines to drive each rear wheel low down in the frame so that a box body seating at least 40 passengers could be provided. At this time the Twin Coaches used Hercules engines of 56 kW (75 bhp) together giving an output greater than any single automobile engine then available. The unladen weight of the vehicle was 7 tons. By 1935 a single 112 kW (150 bhp) engine became available which reduced the advantage of the twin-engined system.

In 1934 Yellow Coach acquired a patent which enabled a bus engine to be placed transversely across the back and a large number of these vehicles were placed in service in New York, and by 1937 buses with engines placed in the conventional front position were no longer made by Yellow Coach.

By 1947 the general size of standard buses in the United States was 10·67 m (35 ft) long and 2·44 m (8 ft) wide. About ten years later the vehicles were 12·2 m (40 ft) long, seating between 40 and 50 with another 50 per cent able to stand.

The Mack Company produced the C50 bus in 1948 to the requirements of the New York Board of Transportation (now the New York City Transit Authority). This was an all-steel integral bus of 12 m by 2·44 m (39 ft 7 in by 8 ft). The unladen weight of the bus was 9½ tons. The power unit was a 6-cylinder vertical diesel engine, built by Mack, mounted in the rear with transmission to the back axle obtained through a hydraulic torque convertor.

A Flxible rear-engined coach in the service of Carey Transportation
in 1951. Flxible, in 1941, had adopted the sloping or parallelogram
styling for the windows which subsequently became a feature of
American bus design.

The Greyhound supercoach built by General Motors utilizing the rear engine design. About 600 of these buses had been built by 1942 when the war stopped production. Between 1946 and 1948 a further 2,000 were built, this time with diesel engines.

The last double-deckers to be built in North America for city operation were built in 1936 for New York and Chicago. They were nicknamed 'Queen Mary's' and had rear engines and a forward stairway.

Power steering as well as power-operated entrance and exit doors was provided. Fluorescent lighting was also fitted to this bus as a standard arrangement, the first time this had been fitted to a fleet of buses. Scania-Vabis of Sweden acquired the rights to manufacture this bus particularly for Stockholm where until the advent of this vehicle the length had been limited to 10·67 m (35 ft).

City buses are generally provided with two doorways, electrically, hydraulically or pneumatically operated with one-man operation universal, usually with a flat fare system. Passengers are required to board at the front entrance, placing the fare in a glass-sided box in full view of the driver. The passenger then passes down the vehicle and leaves when necessary by the rear door which normally opens automatically after being set by the driver as the passenger moves on to the first step. Sometimes on the longer distance routes zone fares apply and usually the buses used on these routes have only one doorway power-operated so that the passenger is required to leave and enter by the driver.

The fourth type of bus which exists in large numbers is the School Bus, which is generally austere in character, a utility type body placed on a truck chassis so that any manufacturer's commercial vehicle can be used and there are many types in use.

They range in size from 12-seaters for handicapped children to 78-seaters.

The exploitation of petroleum began in Texas many years ago, and fuel for internal combustion engines has always been cheap on the American Continent, it has been taxed much less than in Europe and other parts of the world. Thus fuel consumption and weight reduction to achieve better performance has never been critical in the design of American buses, but this factor has encouraged the use of the private car to the exclusion of public transport so that large numbers of children have to travel considerable distances to school daily without the benefit of public transport, so a school bus service has to be provided either by the local authority, school authorities, private operators or parent associations, depending on the local circumstances. However, whoever owns or provides the service, there is usually one thing in common—the buses are all painted bright yellow and are provided with other distinguishing marks including red flashing lights since in most States it is an offence to pass a school bus in either direction when these lights are flashing.

Once the school bus is available, it is often used for private hire purposes for local requirements, such as outings connected with church or old age pensioners' clubs. There are 150,000 school buses

This is the Flxible design of city bus now operating in New York. The air suspension system is used to provide a 'kneeling-action' to reduce the step level for passengers entering the vehicle — a requirement to assist the handicapped. Note the continuation of the parallelogram window design.

The very latest GM city bus with large windows treated for glare but with good visibility — something which was in short supply in most buses in the United States. This vehicle has air suspension, rear engine and power-operated doors but individual operators have little choice in specification except the colour scheme.

in the USA since every community, even in remote areas, has at least one such vehicle and Los Angeles, for example, has several hundred.

Apart from the school buses, it should be remembered that there are as many public service buses in Britain for 50 million inhabitants as there are in the United States for 170 million. The Greyhound fleet, which covers the whole of the United States and part of Canada, owns less than 5,000 vehicles which is less than that owned by London Transport.

The inter-city bus services in America are now dominated by two large concerns, the Greyhound Corporation which is an integrated network owned by a central organization, and the Continental Trailways, an organization which is more of an Association of separate companies with a common buying, publicity and management policy.

In 1936 the Yellow Coach section of the General Motors organization produced the new Super Coach, known as the 'Cruiser' for Greyhound, which had air-conditioning and the engine at the rear, with large luggage space provided underneath the passenger space. By 1939, some 1,600 of these buses were operating for Greyhound and its associated companies. At the New York World's Fair of 1940 the new and improved Yellow super coach known as 'Silversides' made its first appearance. Some 60 cm (2 ft) larger than the Cruiser it was constructed mainly of aluminium to reduce weight and fitted with a diesel engine at the rear instead of a petrol (gasoline) engine. This vehicle seats 37 passengers.

The 'Scenicruiser' first appeared in 1949. This was a split-level bus of 3-axle design and 12·2 m (40 ft) length. Most of the seats were fitted in the upper level together with a toilet and it had an exceptionally large baggage compartment. In addition to the fitting of air-conditioning this was the first large scale design which used air suspension, providing a better and smoother ride. By 1953 air suspension was provided as a standard fitment to all General Motors buses and by 1957 all Greyhound long-distance buses were provided with toilet facilities. The Scenicruiser had a dual engine installation with the final drive through a fluid coupling linking the output of both engines to a single transmission. Thus two 4-cylinder engines provided the equivalent of an 8-cylinder engine without the engineering balancing difficulties inherent in the larger engine.

Flxible produced a competitive design which the Trailways organization sponsored, this was a 10·67 m (35 ft) long 37-passenger vehicle on 4 wheels, also with a split-level arrangement. This vehicle was known as the Vista Liner and was provided with a Cummins diesel engine.

A school bus on an International chassis with a typical austerity type body. School buses are constructed on many types of commercial chassis.

Buses which cross State boundaries plying for hire require a licence in each State and through-buses are festooned with licence plates. Greyhound and Trailways, in particular, have to segregate their fleets into zones of operation to cover this requirement.

The long-distance operators are permitted the same speed limits as private cars. These regulations are applied by the different states, but in recent times as a fuel economy measure the maximum speed is rarely in excess of 89 km/h (55 mph).

There is no charting (booking) of bus seats on long-distance routes because the regulations generally permit up to one-third standing of the seating available. However, it is most unusual for passengers to have to stand from a 'control' or stopping point, because spare vehicles are retained to back up scheduled services. Heavy luggage is checked from point to point and not handled by passengers after making a through-booking, a practice operated by both the railways and the airways in America.

There is another large organization which operates touring and sightseeing services in most cities of the United States, known as the Gray Line. This too is an association which provides a kind of franchise to a local operator to use the Gray Line fleet name and advertising publicity and in return provides various management functions. Greyhound in fact has this franchise in some cities—San Francisco, for example, but can be in competition for sightseeing tours in others with another operator with the Gray Line franchise. The Gray Line tours have a worldwide reputation with travel agents.

Miscellany

There is an infinite variety of vehicles used for public service not only in Britain, but in all parts of the world. The following examples illustrate some of the odds and ends which have been provided for the conveyance of fare-paying passengers under many different circumstances.

During the fuel shortage of World War I, town gas was used. The gas was stored in balloons carried on the roofs of the vehicles. Shown is a Lothian of the Scottish Motor Traction Co. in Edinburgh modified to operate in this way.

In World War II producer gas generators were towed behind vehicles to enable gas to be used instead of petrol. Over 500 ST type double-decker buses were converted in London and other types in other parts of Britain, but fuel supply did not become so desperate that extensive conversion programmes were introduced.

A number of seaside resorts introduced 'toastracks' for trips along promenades and scenic holiday routes. Shelroke and Drewry, the constructors of mechanical refuse collectors, provided many of these vehicles. In 1938 this example was used by Crosville on the Welsh Coast resorts.

A coachbuilder (Gottlob Auwarter) of Stuttgart, Germany, produced a chassis-less integral rear-engined bus in 1953 which was named Neoplan. A double-decker version, seating 102 passengers, was exhibited at the Munich Transport Exhibition in 1965. This vehicle was based on Büssing-NAG chassis components. The basic Neoplan designs have since been exported to many parts of the world for construction under licence including America. Touring buses with sleeping accommodation have also been constructed on this basic design.

A Ford Transit minibus for special services provided by London Transport. Seating for 16 is provided in a length under 2·74 m (9 ft).

In several cities in the world there is a need for small-capacity buses, Volkswagen have catered for the market, especially in South America where a factory has been established to build them. This type of operation in Caracas is referred to as a 'jitney' since it is often in opposition to the established operator. The term 'jitney' was coined in the United States in the early 1920s when similar limousine competition at low fares was being felt by the established street car operators in many cities.

A Leyland Comet tractor with double-decker trailer for service in India. When large capacity vehicles are required this can be a solution to the problem.

In the 1960s Zurich Transport in Switzerland began operating a small fleet of FBW type buses with the driver in an elevated position with a clear view of the road ahead. The design, however, was not repeated.

Where to see buses in Britain

There are now a number of bus preservation societies in various parts of Britain. These societies not only own many buses which they are preserving in original condition but encourage and help individual members to acquire vehicles of their own. These societies also organize rallies and nostalgic runs for their members and friends which are enjoyed by all those interested in buses.

There are, however, a number of transport museums which have among the items in their collections buses of various kinds which can be inspected at any time the museums are open to the public—the most important of these collections are listed below.

Belfast Transport Museum
Witham Street
Newtownards Road
Belfast, BT4 1HP

Bournemouth Transport and Rural Museum
Mallard Road Depot
Bournemouth, Dorset

Bury Transport Museum
Castlecroft Road
Bury, Greater Manchester
BL9 0LN

Cobham Bus Museum
Redhill Road, Cobham
Surrey, KT11 1EF

East Anglia Transport Museum
Chapel Road, Carlton Colville
Lowestoft, Suffolk

East Pennine Transport Group
Spring Street, Marsden
Huddersfield, HD7 6HE

Glasgow Museum of Transport
25 Albert Drive, Coplawhill
Glasgow, G41 2PE

Gough's Motor and Transport Museum
The Cliffs, Cheddar, Somerset

Hull Transport Museum
36 High Street
Kingston-upon-Hull
Humberside

Leicestershire Museum of Technology
Abbey Pumping Station
Corporation Road
Leicester, LE4 5PX

London Transport Museum
39 Wellington Street
London, WC2E 7BB

Midland Bus Museum
Wythall, Bromsgrove
Birmingham

The Museum of British Road Transport
Cook Street, Coventry
West Midlands

Museum of Transport
Boyle Street, Cheetham
Greater Manchester, M8 8UW

National Motor Museum
Beaulieu, Hampshire
SO4 7ZN

Sandtoft Transport Centre
Sandtoft, Near Doncaster
South Yorkshire

Transport Museum Society of Ireland
Donart, County Wicklow
Ireland

INDEX

Source Books

Aircraft
Armoured Fighting Vehicles
Buses
Commercial Vehicles
Dinghies
Helicopters and Vertical Take-Off Aircraft
Hydrofoils and Hovercraft
Industrial Past
Locomotives
Military Support Vehicles
Miniature and Narrow Gauge Railways
Motor Cars
Motorcycles
Naval Aircraft and Aircraft Carriers
Ships
Small Arms
Submarines and Submersibles
Tractors and Farm Machinery
Trams
Twentieth Century Warships
Underground Railways
Veteran Cars
Vintage and Post Vintage Cars
Windmills and Watermills
World War 1 Weapons and Uniforms
World War 2 Weapons and Uniforms